FOLKER KRUEGER

WELL REMEMBERED

A KALEIDOSCOPE OF SHORT STORIES

Copyright © Folker Krueger, 2023

This book is sold subject to the condition that it shall not, by way of trade or otherwise, be lent, resold, hired out, or otherwise circulated without the Publisher's prior consent in any form of binding or cover other than that in which it is published and without a similar condition including this condition being imposed on the subsequent publisher.

The moral right of Folker Krueger (the author and publisher) has been asserted.

ISBN 978-0-646-88170-6
First published in September 2023
Photography: Folker Krueger and others
Design: Mich Lee
Illustration: Alastair Taylor · www.goatpix.com

My memoir, The Lottery of Life, was published in 2016.

On reflection, I realised that there are many more stories to be told.

I do hope you will enjoy my recollections of past events; I have found that a funny twist in life makes it so much more interesting.

Happy reading…

Indonesia was our home for nearly nine years. Work dominated daily life, including the frequent social events, which provided a perfect platform to network within the business community.

The activities of the Indonesian-Australian Business Council and the German Chamber of Commerce blended in with very popular social events conducted by the Chaine des Rotisseurs and the Jakarta Wine and Spirit Society. In addition, golf became a regular feature on weekends, to such an extent that a friend and I started a German Golf Tournament, which became the second most valuable tournament in Indonesia in terms of sponsorship. Finally, I conducted a bi-monthly Happy Hour, intending to provide a venue for the German business community to get together and socialise to exchange views on the current issues in Indonesia, which affected all of us.

Patrons of these events included prominent people in Indonesia, including several ambassadors from various countries like Germany, Australia, Chile and Cuba.

In our company, the staff became a close team. Due to them, we have been able to show a steady improvement in profits, even during the difficult times of the political upheavals in Indonesia during the years 1997/1998.

When I prepared a farewell party for 150 people, all of that weighed on my mind. It was just before my transfer from Jakarta to Perth, WA, in 2004.

Our regional director from Singapore attended. All senior staff were invited. They honoured all the guests by wearing their traditional Indonesian attire. Our local partner and the top management presented me with a gift of 36 bottles of Australian wines, to be collected in Perth when I settled into my new abode.

My farewell speech tried to address all the different people I met during my years in Jakarta. Of course, that was an impossible task, but here is what I had to say.

Farewell speech Jakarta, 2004

Excellencies, Ladies and Gentlemen, Friends – not as a separate group but meaning all of you!

There is one other group, though, represented by my golfing buddies. But since they are always picking on me, laughing at me and even shooting better scores than me, how can I call them friends?

I am glad they are here as they can see that I am not such a bad guy, and they can mix and meet some of the civilised population of this town.

When our Regional Director, Mr Karl Heinz Matthes, and our President Director of PT, Schenker Petrolog Utama, spoke such kind words about me, I became emotional and mushy inside.

But, since I have known them both for quite some time, I know that they always speak the truth. Since the truth, this time, was also accompanied by such an appreciated gift, how can you argue with the truth? NOT ME! Thank you very much, both of you.

Looking back over the 8 ½ years, I must say that we had some bad times and many good times. Did I mention golf?

Some of you may feel that it is not an easy country to work in and live in? You are all wrong! The problem with you is most likely that you think you know the right way of doing things, and that is the first mistake. Next, you get upset about little things which will not change your life. You are still upset when you get home, which is the second mistake. Your private life suffers; you carry your perceived burdens into your family circle.

My recipe has been straightforward. I did not come here as a missionary (lots of those ended up in the cooking pot in the past). I saw my task as to work the best I could with the resources I had, train myself and my staff to take the next step and hope that H.O. would have the patience to follow me.

In between (and sometimes more often), go out and enjoy yourself. But not too much, as this tends to be very tiring too.

As you can see by my shape, I did not have too much time to do sports. Golf is not quite enough, although mentally, it is considered one of the best exercises.

My survival instinct led me into the arms of the Chaine des Rotisseurs, where good food is the order of the day. To keep up with the fluids in this tropical climate, I also spend many hours trying to fathom the intricacies of the fabulous wines of this world in the Wine and Spirit Circle. Both organisations helped to keep me in shape, and I am grateful for the good times we had together.

This is a business function, so I suppose I should talk about that a little, but I cannot divide my private life and friends from business life. Both have the same basic ingredients that make them work.

Communication, understanding of each other (even if one has differences in opinions) and, most importantly, trust. To me, those are the most critical cornerstones which work in business, with friends and with your marriage.

On the golf course, it is easier. You play one round, and you know the character of the partner you play with. But, often, totally different behaviour is displayed on the course, which makes you think: do I really know this guy?

You do not have to make emergency arrangements in that situation, but it helps to establish who is who.

It's slightly different in management. I sometimes compare actions to be taken by management with my past activities as a gliding instructor.

You train a guy on how to fly. You take him up in the air, talk to him and hope he talks back. That's what is called communication. You know through his communication what he may think or what he considers. You increase your trust in him slowly until you reach the point where you decide to let him take responsibility. The litmus test comes at 1,000 feet above ground at a critical distance from the landing field. One wrong action would make you crash land. How far can you trust this guy? How experienced is he really? That is a management decision, so if necessary, you take the joystick yourself and head in the right direction, even if it might take a few more tight turns to keep afloat until you can land safely.

There are many parallels in the daily business scene. If you make a mistake as a manager, it will not show immediately in a crash landing but will show up in the P/L Report without fail. The decision-making ability under pressure creates trust in a leader, and I like to think that I may have successfully built a team in this company that has grown together on those principles.

The success of this company, small as it is, has directly resulted from teamwork. Our managers and staff tried hard to follow my guidance and achieve results they could only dream of some years ago.

A big thank you to our partner, Mr MP, who has guided me on many occasions regarding local systems and mentality and who has kept me sane in sometimes mad surroundings. Also, a thank you to all my staff who helped build the company into what it is today, but there is also a threat—if you do not keep up the excellent work, I will come back!

I also want to thank my wife, Rosita, for the support she has given me in fulfilling my tasks.

It was difficult to adjust to a new country, experience the turbulent times in 1998 and keep smiling. And that she has done a lot, the life of the party, and through her friends, I got into a fantastic circle of people who made me look even older than I am.

Last but not least, I want to thank our clients for their support, even though it may have been difficult at times, as I am not in the habit of mincing words. It was great to be of service whenever possible, and I will miss the challenges you have thrown at me from time to time.

This is not a wake; I am not retiring, just relocation. I will try to work as Product Manager in Asia in the Project and Oil & Gas sector. Based in Perth, WA but attached to the RHO in Singapore, can life get any better?

This is a reason to celebrate, and that's what we intend to do tonight.

I'll talk to you later; let's have some food and wine to settle the butterflies in the stomach. "

A Night Visitor

The consistent banging on my bedroom door finally woke me up. It was after midnight, and I was alone in the main part of our house in Jakarta; my wife was travelling overseas. Who on earth was making that racket? Slowly, I realised that our housemaid was urgently calling out to me to come and investigate an attempt to enter our property by force. Our home was a sprawling old house situated in a small side lane in a suburb south of Jakarta. The entrance to our place was locked off with an ornate iron gate. To achieve privacy from gawking passers-by, the landlord had covered the entire gate with light coloured, rigid plastic sheeting.

Obviously, our maid, Suyatmi, was afraid; her husband-cum-gardener was cowering in the background, useless for any serious action.

I was lightly dressed, as the heat and humidity could be stifling in that city. There was no way I was getting dressed up in my finery just to kick a possible burglar out of our premises. Exiting via the kitchen and side entrance, I could already hear yelling and shouting from the gate, and it seemed some damage had been done to the plastic sheets. A fist was punching through the sheets, repeatedly trying to reach the gate lock from the inside.

As we had been advised, Jakarta was not exactly a safe place. After arrival in Indonesia, one of my first purchases was a metal baseball bat, which always rested near my bedside at night. Not being a trained fighter, I took a little confidence from that bat in my hand as I approached the front gate.

Something was not right. Obscenities and abuse were being hurled at me, but the agitated voice was female. To prevent further damage to our front gate by this constant punching, I decided to open up to confront the person, baseball bat in hand.

I think the woman in front of me and I were both surprised. She was a large individual, Caucasian, and I estimated she was not older than 35 years. She only had a nightgown to cover her up, and she looked dishevelled. I suppose that she would have looked relatively attractive when cleaned up.

Her facial expression was one of great shock at seeing me. Her shouting stopped. She looked at me again, and I was not sure what her next step would be. Meanwhile, we accumulated onlookers in the form of the neighbouring local population of night watchmen, or fellows who just smoked and drank the night away with their friends, enjoying the cooler air at night. I was not sure what my housemaid and her husband were thinking of all this. It became clear that the lady in front of me was totally intoxicated and had forgotten how to act like a lady, except when she realised she did not know me. She started to cry and almost collapsed on the street. To cut the drama, I dragged her into our compound, closed the gate and sat her on a bench outside our kitchen. I asked her repeatedly who she was, where she came from and what she wanted at my house. The best way to describe her state was highly drunk, incoherent, and mentally in upheaval. The gist of her bubbling seemed to be that she was sorry to visit my house, sorry to create such a disturbance, and I could not agree more. I tried to ask her where she was living and gathered it was nearby, a couple of lanes away. She could not give me the address or a telephone number, but said she would find it when she walked back. I have not been called a gentleman without reason in the past, but I was also very curious. To make sure she got home safely, I insisted on accompanying her; passing the many local night travellers, alone, in her state, would have been a haunting experience. At least that was what I reasoned, although she was in no condition to understand that. The sight must have been something to behold. A middle-aged man in sleeping attire almost dragged a big, pyjama-clad woman through the back lanes of Jakarta. A spectacle to be discussed for weeks by anybody who watched us, and there were many.

We made it. About ten minutes later, we arrived at what she claimed was her house. She managed to open the gate and front door and asked me inside; we left the sniggering local street dwellers behind. I felt pretty safe; she certainly was not capable of doing me any physical harm because she could hardly stand up.

She sat down and slowly came out of the cloud she had been floating in before. I offered to make her a cup of tea, since I gathered she was from Australia, and my experience was that in that country, tea was considered medicine to cure all sorts of ailments.

Slowly, her story emerged. She and her partner were running their own business, seemingly quite successful. When the inevitable happened, and her partner found another young lady to comfort him, the business suffered, and the relationship became somewhat toxic. That night she was drinking alone at home until her jealousy became unbearable. She decided to visit the house where she suspected the unholy liaison was taking place. Alcohol is not a good navigator. She ended up in front of my house, thinking she had found the den where her partner had his own entertainment. The following action came from her heart, shouting and yelling abuse at him and starting to demolish my front gate.

I think she finally realised what had happened, and she started sobbing again, this time out of embarrassment. All I could do was give her my telephone number in case she needed help and suggested she have a rest before going on any other excursions. At that stage, I still could not get her to give me her name; she was probably so ashamed of her behaviour that she preferred to stay anonymous.

My good deed done, I staggered back to my house to catch up on a couple of hours' sleep before having to face work again in the office. I apologised to the staff at home for the disturbance but assured them I had never met the lady before, that I did not know who she was and that nothing was going on between us. Maybe they did not believe me, but there was nothing I could do about it. I just needed more sleep.

I never heard from the lady in question again and presumed she was doing OK after sobering up.

A few months later, my wife and I attended a social gathering in the home of an Australian friend when I saw this young lady again. Laughing, smiling, a drink in her hand, chatting away with a group of people. Being polite, I nodded a friendly hello to her, but there was not a glimmer of recognition. Just as well; I definitely did not want to gain notoriety by being discussed by the gossiping ladies and men of the expat community in Jakarta.

There is a myth about children who have grown up living the life of an expat. The most common view is that they have been born with a silver spoon in their mouth; they are spoiled and do not understand life's values. Servants make things easier for the parents, but the children take it for granted and spend their time being cared for, day and night. What happens when that life ends and they have to return home?

The Story

It all started with the necessity of earning a living. The mother was Australian. Her German husband had tried to survive in Australia as a migrant with limited success. It is not unusual to lose a job, and finding employment that could provide for the future is essential. Unfortunately, an interim solution did not last very long because of disputes within the employer's family, and the future looked bleak once again. To make things worse, the first baby was born, and little Casper had already had a poor start. Born six weeks early, the little infant had to begin his journey with a stint in an incubator, and he came out fighting. Father Kurt had many worries, and it wasn't easy to enjoy the first year of his son's existence.

Desperate, Kurt placed an advertisement in a German paper catering to the professional interests of companies engaged in the transport industry. Not long after, Kurt got an invitation to attend an interview in Hong Kong for the country director position of a German/Swiss company in Taiwan. All went well, and they agreed to start the new career by attending a six-week introduction course in their big hub in Frankfurt. The wife's parents gave the young family shelter in Sydney for the duration and joined Kurt several weeks later in Taipei.

The search for suitable accommodation took longer than expected, and the little family lived in The Grand Hotel in Taipei for nearly three months. It was rather cramped, but it was an excellent opportunity to look for a more permanent place to live whilst Kurt had to get to grips with the new challenges in a strange country. Finally, they found a house, somewhat large, but since a maid was included, it did not look too much of a task to keep the household going.

Life settled down, club memberships helped them to integrate quickly, and the wife, Rebecca, took to it with gusto. They made many friends, held parties at home and in the club, tennis was on the agenda, and it all looked comfortable. The maid was an elderly Taiwanese lady with a sour face, but she was outstanding in keeping the place tidy, looked after Casper, and was a great help to have around. Taiwan was a very safe place to live, as, officially, they still had martial law in place because of the continuing threat from mainland China just a short distance away across the China Sea. Western-style food was limited, but since the country had a powerful presence in the American military, they had access to some goodies they sold in the military supermarkets. It was illegal, but soldiers supplemented their income by buying food in their shops and selling it to the local entrepreneurs, who made it available to civilian expats, albeit at a higher price.

Casper enjoyed Chinese food, and restaurants were abundant. However, the parents noticed Casper began to develop strong tendencies of hyperactivity by the time he was three years old. It took some time to get information on the syndrome, through a group of Australian women who were very helpful. Various suggestions were made, and a test showed that the condition got worse every time Casper was exposed to noisy surroundings, foodstuffs containing phosphorus and sweets.

Going to a Chinese Restaurant showed that Casper's behaviour changed as soon as the place filled up with other guests. The Chinese tend to be very noisy at their gatherings. Little Casper became agitated and started running around the tables, lost concentration, and often bumped himself on the furniture. Many food items were tested. Slowly, a picture formed of what had to be done to reduce the external effects so that Casper was considered a sweet and well-behaved boy. No mean task.

But the expat life posed a few hurdles. Many mothers organised birthday parties for their kids, and everybody was invited. The children who did not have a birthday all received a little goody bag stuffed with sweets, chocolates and similar items. Not the sort of diet Casper should enjoy. To make him feel better, he was taught to bring home these items, which were almost poisonous to him. He could sample a few choice items on the weekend, when he could run around in a safer environment. That would practically become a circus. Casper had his own little room with iron safety guards on the windows, and a large net was installed over his bed to protect him from mosquitoes. Many nights, the parents were woken up by loud noises from Casper's room. After a few good hours of sleep, he would get busy and climb the iron structure on his window and drop on top of his mosquito net to use it as a swing, letting out very loud shouts of joy. Needless to say, this was hazardous, as the net was attached only to small hooks on the ceiling, and an accident could easily have happened. It took some time to calm him down and get him back to sleep, and obviously, the night's rest was ruined for the parents.

Casper claimed he liked animals. The first indication was that he started collecting many caterpillars in the garden, which he transported to his bedroom in his toy truck to play with. But unfortunately, these little beasts had long, hairy bodies that shed things when cuddled by a little boy. Itches and wheezing were the results, and that excursion into animal husbandry was stopped smartly.

Not to be outdone, Casper discovered a bat, which had become stuck on the tape around the window's air-conditioner. He loved the look of the small, cute animal and tried to release it from its confinement, only to be bitten by the bat's small, sharp teeth. What a disappointment to Casper, as he only wanted to show his love for little living things.

The grandparents came for a visit from Sydney. They suggested investing in a trampoline, which was the best thing to tire the guy out, give him a feeling of freedom, and improve his coordination skills, to prevent him from bumping into furniture during his more excited phases.

Life went on, and Casper and his parents fell into some sort of disciplined routine, which gave both parties less trouble by introducing some normality into their social life. In addition, the interaction with peers helped to get Casper interested in learning activities, although his concentration faded quickly, and new ideas had to be introduced frequently to keep him occupied.

Other excitement was not so well received. Taiwan is part of the Ring of Fire in the Pacific Region and experiences earthquakes from time to time. The feeling of the ground shaking and the swimming pool water swamping over the side turned out not to be an enjoyable experience. Luckily, this happened only a few times and was quickly forgotten.

Another quirk of nature is the typhoons or cyclones, as they are called in the Western world. During the summer months, 12 or 13 typhoons would form in the south; most hit the Philippines and then travel north to Taiwan, Hong Kong and Japan or turn to the other side, crossing towards

Vietnam. Taiwan is spared the strongest typhoons most of the time, but plenty of wind and rain are experienced regularly.

Rebecca was pregnant again. Regular visits to a local doctor ensured everything went smoothly. In time, a hospital bed was booked for the estimated delivery date, as there was an issue with hospital space in Taipei. A few days before the big day, the weather forecast showed a typhoon on its way to Taiwan. On coming closer, it formed into a super-typhoon with predicted extreme winds and rain. You can't stop a baby from coming into this world, so they took the trip to the hospital, and told the doctor to get there on time. Mothers are not at their best during such times, and she became somewhat agitated when she inspected the hospital room.

The room was small and damp, and the bed linen was every shade of grey. To make things worse, the linen had several sizeable holes, and another layer of linen was put over the original ones to cover those up. Being the daughter of a GP, she was very concerned about hygiene and refused to give birth in that room. Nothing else was available in the hospital, and after the doctor arrived, one hour late, a conference started about what to do. The doctor had a financial interest in a private hospital not so far away and suggested going there to check in. There was no other choice, so Kurt drove to the new hospital in the increasing rain and wind.

This establishment was also fully booked, but the doctor miraculously got the last room offered to Kurt at an exorbitant price. It was a suite with two rooms, very comfortable. Still, as a private hospital that did not have official approval from the government, the medical insurance would not cover the costs. Knowing the system by then, Kurt negotiated the price.

Meanwhile, Rebecca was holding her belly and making strange noises. That was not a great help in reducing costs. A financially unsatisfactory agreement was reached so Rebecca could finally be admitted and made comfortable.

Outside the hospital in central Taipei, strong winds were howling. Inside, Rebecca was whimpering and demanded a 'cocktail' to ease the pain and speed up the delivery. She got her wish, and a baby girl was born just two hours later.

Kurt was not very good at distinguishing between babies, but it was made easier since all the other new arrivals that night looked very Chinese. There was that little bundle looking all scrunched up, but it had the required number of toes and fingers; all was fine. After one day's rest and supervision, the family moved back home, where the maid and Casper awaited the new arrival.

They had to choose a name from a long list prepared months before, and Kurt had little to say in this matter; the baby girl was called Melissa. Greek mythology has several versions of a Nymph who saved the life of one of the gods by giving him a concoction of honey and water, which seemed to work; hence, the name Melissa has also been associated with the honey bee.

Meanwhile, the typhoon arrived, and the house was boarded up with planks, and plastic tape on the windows to prevent serious damage in case they were blown in. Unfortunately, the damage to the infrastructure also meant the electricity was cut for nearly three days, presenting more problems with cooking and limiting them to survival with minimum comforts. The maid kept busy boiling water on a fondue cooker to get sterile water to wash Melissa on the kitchen table by candlelight.

When the winds and heavy rain subsided, it was time to look around the house to see what had happened. The swimming pool was overflowing, full of leaves and branches stripped off the hedge alongside the walls. It was pure luck that there was a low-lying road at the back of the house, where the water could flow down without flooding the house. The cleaning-up process took several days, with some help from hired hands.

Kurt was worried about his offices. The Taipei branch was OK, with no damage, although no work took place for three days as all staff had to shelter at home during that period. The branch in Kaohsiung port could not be contacted, as all telephone lines were down. Still, after two days, the news was received that everybody there was OK. Unfortunately, the port was a total mess. Heavy container cranes were blown over, partially blocking the quay. Stacked containers were toppled on the ground, and the operation was severely restricted in the coming weeks. It was really amazing to witness what winds and rain can do; the fury of the elements seemed to have no boundaries.

The first drive to the office in Taipei resembled an obstacle race. Broken tree branches and telephone lines were strewn over the road; some roads were still flooded, but the advantage was that there was little traffic on the way.

Slowly, life in Taipei settled back into routine, and the population took everything in their stride; most people had similar experience from previous events.

Little Casper had to get used to the fact that there was a new attention seeker in the house. Barely three years old, he was fascinated with the process of changing nappies and feeding the baby, and soon he realised that this would change part of his life forever. Not to be outdone, he soon returned to his little world and got a fair bit of attention whenever he was up to his antics again.

Kurt missed out on many family activities because of the strong demands imposed by his position in the company. Taiwan citizens were not allowed to travel outside the country, which meant that he had to undertake the overseas trips. Frequent travels inside Taiwan and overseas kept him away for many days. On returning, he had to catch up with the latest little dramas in his household. Luckily, Rebecca was quite sociable and made many friends who also had children of similar ages. Playgroups were formed, which entertained the kids and mothers alike. The American Club became the hub of many of those activities, including lively tennis matches right under the flight path of the city airport. Often, you could see players duck down as it seemed the aircraft coming in over the top were trying to take the roof off the building. The noise created by the aircraft was disturbing for Casper, but he also developed an interest in big things that could fly; it was much more interesting than watching bugs and insects.

After two years, the contract for the house was about to expire. The landlord had this weird notion that money grew on trees for the expat community and increased the rent considerably; that was not acceptable. A new house had to be found, which meant moving further out from the city, to Wellington Heights, which was a larger housing enclave hugging a hillside in Peitou. A short street on top of the hill had only eight larger houses, built alongside a famous temple, which was commonly called the Love Temple. Young local couples visited there to pray and hope for good luck for their future. By strange coincidence, four other Germans lived on the same street. The manager of Hapag Lloyd shipping line on the right, and on the left was a gentleman running the Taipei office of the big German mail-order house, Quelle. Next to him was the manager of Lufthansa. It was a pleasant neighbourhood, and they developed a good social life, resulting in some lifelong friendships.

They often went on outings on Sundays, weather permitting. Yangmingshan was a popular destination, on top of the hills, where one could go for walks and enjoy the view down towards Taipei. Two blond children provided some excitement for the local population. Since blond was considered equivalent to gold, they all tried to touch the hair of Casper and Melissa for good luck. That upset Casper frequently, but Melissa enjoyed the attention. The afternoon's highlight was the promised treat of fruit and ice cream. The café proudly offered this Western-style delight to attract more foreigners and locals to their place. A lot of research must have gone into the menu, and technically, the concoction delivered what it promised; fruit and ice cream. Nobody can argue that tomatoes are not a fruit, but the combination with ice cream did not quite come up to the expectation of the little experts. The pleasant afternoon ended as somewhat of a disappointment for the kids.

A significant part of the life of a manager was to look after overseas visitors, resulting in many evenings away from home. One night Kurt attended a dinner for his regional finance director. Fortunately, on this occasion, he only had a couple of beers before reverting to orange juice because of the long drive home. To cut out traffic, he chose a back road, which followed the dyke holding back the Dan Sui (Tamsui) River on one side and endless rice paddies on the other. Kurt was driving towards a single light coming his way at speed, weaving back and forth, and it was not clear where the motorbike was heading. He was hugging the road within the confines of the white lines when the motorbike suddenly swerved to his side, impacting on the car at full speed. The force of the crash pushed the car slightly across the centre line, and the bumper bar was dented badly, even though Kurt was driving only at around 20 km per hour at that stage. The next seconds were blurred.

A body flew over the car, a second man ended up on the roadside moaning, and the motorbike was badly damaged. Efforts to stop other road users to get help were useless. The general attitude then was not to get involved at all. Finally, Kurt hitched a ride into town to call on the special foreign police office for help. The police car, with two officers and Kurt, sped back to the scene, to find only the car and the motorbike left. From bystanders, the police learned that ambulance chasers had picked up the two riders and taken them to a local private hospital. On arrival, they could see that one man had been roughly dumped into another ambulance for transportation to a bigger, better-equipped government hospital. The second guy was looked after in the private hospital and could not be interviewed, but it seemed that he had only suffered a broken leg. The police drove Kurt back to his car and helped with bending back the bent metal so he could drive home. It was already after midnight, and the next morning Kurt had to give an explanation to his children about why he did not come home on time. Luckily, they did not understand the dire circumstances and happily waved goodbye to him when he left to inspect the accident scene in daylight.

The traffic was still light when Kurt visited the site of the crash. It was easy to move around and look for indications of what may have occurred. The motorbike had been moved and now rested against the wall of the dyke. Somewhat shortened through the impact, it was also covered with mud, showing that it had taken a prior diversion into one of the rice paddies. There was some blood on the road, and a clear tyre mark showing Kurt's efforts to brake just before impact. The rubber skid mark just crossing the centre line showed the force of the crash. Pictures of all the visible facts, including the damage incurred by the car, became useful later when the drama unfolded.

It only took a few hours, and the police requested Kurt to attend the Government Hospital, where one of the accident victims was being treated. The family surrounded the bed, and the doctor and a couple of nurses explained that the man was brain-dead and they intended to switch off the life support. But first, the family forced Kurt to touch the hand of the person in bed; it was still warm. Then for comparison, he had to touch one foot which appeared cold, which meant nothing but seemed to be calculated intimidation by the victim's family. Finally, the doctor explained what had happened. The high-speed impact of the motorcycle sent this person flying over the car only to land on his head, which was not protected by a helmet. The resulting injuries were severe, and the private hospital could not deal with them and passed the patient on to a well-equipped establishment. To no avail, as had become apparent.

A couple of days later, Kurt was requested to attend a Coroners hearing at the hospital morgue. The victim's family was all present, the Coroner insisted on pulling the body out of the freezer, and a photographer was busy taking pictures of the naked man on the slab. Not a pleasant sight, but it revealed several tattoos on the body, which generally meant some connection or membership to a gang.

Regardless, the verdict of the Coroner was manslaughter, and Kurt was the person accused of that crime.

The police were required to take Kurt into custody and present him to a Magistrates Court to get him released on bail. Since the police seemed to be short of transport, Kurt drove them to court, accompanied by the CFO of the company, to have a witness and translator present. The friendly court officials suggested waiting for a little because the Magistrate was very busy. So instead of being put into a holding cell with many other questionable persons, like accused murderers and gangsters, a chair was placed in front of the holding cell, where Kurt had to sit and wait before his appointment with the Magistrate. It was not a very comfortable situation, but since he had a bunch of chewing gum in his pocket, he shared this with the wretched characters behind bars to break the ice. Not that this resulted in a lively conversation, as none of those other inmates could speak English, but the atmosphere became less hostile.

After a short hearing in front of the Magistrate, Kurt was released on bail on his own recognizance, and the stern advice of the legal god in charge was to settle a civil claim for manslaughter with the family first. The civil agreement had to be agreed before the State would judge him on the manslaughter charge.

Kurt's office was full of the deceased family members for the next three weeks, demanding a significant sum of money as compensation. Their son was around 35 years old, and they calculated his ability to earn huge incomes for another 50 years. Although insurance would cover the claim, it was a face-saving necessity that Kurt would also commit his own contribution to show sincerity. The family even threatened to put the corpse on display in front of Kurt's home until he agreed to pay compensation.

On the advice of the insurance company, a settlement was agreed upon, almost ten times more than any known case involving a foreigner in such an accident! A significant reason for this decision was the underlying suggestion that bad things could happen if a satisfactory payment were not received, since the family belonged to a known textile mafia in the South of Taiwan, as confirmed by the tattoos witnessed on the victim during the Coroner's inquest.

The date of the court case was some weeks ahead. Kurt did not trust the local judiciary and looked for help in establishing the facts. A member of his Lions Club was a lawyer who also taught at the police academy. His credentials gave him access to the police file of the accident, and he recorded the essential facts; since it now was official that somebody independent had seen the files, it would be difficult to change or consider deleting details.

A fact-finding meeting took place with the authorities to determine if Kurt should be found guilty. There was a quaint system in case of traffic accidents involving foreigners. Twelve members of the public assembled to discuss the facts and put a recommendation to the court. Teachers and office workers, anybody could be drafted into such a committee; it was not a formal jury selection but had a similar purpose.

Kurt could not bring an interpreter. Nearly one hour of long discussions in Chinese was finally interrupted by Kurt demanding an explanation in English so he could contribute to the debate! The accusation was that Kurt had driven too fast, that he went on the wrong side of the road, causing the accident, and that the deceased was the driver of the motorcycle and his pillion passenger survived with a broken leg and was treated in a private hospital. OK, now at least Kurt knew what to argue. He presented the pictures he had taken at the accident scene and explained. The length of the brake line of the road was used to calculate a speed of around 20 km per hour only. Driving on the wrong side of the road was disproved since only one front wheel was pushed over the centre line by the impact of the accident caused by the motorcycle. The picture of the muddy motorcycle showed that these two riders must have fallen into a rice paddy before continuing their journey. Another strange fact was that the motorcycle had been stolen from the accident scene one day later; the police claimed they did not secure it as evidence. The suggestion was that both riders were totally drunk at the time; they had come from a family gathering on 'tomb sweeping day', which traditionally ends up in a serious drinking session. The doctor in the private hospital claimed he was too busy saving lives, so he did not take any blood samples for alcohol testing.

Kurt was told that the court hearing would be some time away. In the meantime, he needed a break and took the home leave due to him after three years of work. He booked flights to Germany, and a small apartment became available to rent in the village where his mother and brother lived, some 45 km south of Hannover. Nine weeks of continuous holidays was an excellent opportunity for Casper and Melissa to spend some quality time with their grandmother. But that nearly did not happen.

Kurt could not travel until the court conducted the hearing on the accident. It was just hours before departure and he had heard nothing. What to do? The family was ready to move and had packed everything, and the wide-eyed children could not quite follow what was happening. Kurt decided to make another effort at extending his bail conditions. He sent the family ahead to the airport to wait for him before checking in. Kurt rushed to the courthouse and managed to pull a magistrate out from one of his hearings to get a special permit to leave the country.

After considering the circumstances and the assurance that Kurt would return on a fixed date to await the trial, the magistrate granted his request. Kurt drove straight to the airport, knowing it was touch and go to arrive in time for the flight. The family was exhausted from all the tension but finally settled down on the long flight to Germany.

Actually, the children did well. Since airline regulations were still somewhat relaxed and flights were seldom fully booked, Rebecca prepared makeshift beds from blankets and pillows on the floor behind the front seat so the little blighters could sleep. Of course, it helped that they were still very young, slim, and very tired.

It was summer in Germany, and the beautiful surroundings in the village of Lauenstein/Ith worked their magic quickly, so the family could relax together. They took long walks in the forest with grandmother and everybody settled into living in a peaceful place. No traffic, no pollution, plenty of trees and bushes and lots of space to play in, a little paradise after the restrictions of living in a big, foreign city like Taipei. To add to the fun, Kurt had bought a new car directly from the Mercedes factory; he planned to use it during the holidays and sell it again before leaving the country. There was a long waiting list for this type of Mercedes, which had a diesel engine and even a sunroof. That was the basis of the assumption that the vehicle could be sold near the buying price after the holidays.

Lovely excursions to lakes, restaurants serving beautiful smoked eels, and visits to the local gliding club rounded up the daily excitement. Meals cooked at home finished the day, and the peaceful farming surroundings made sleep one of the highlights of every day. Kurt's mother loved the kids.

She had no English skills, but she would entertain the youngsters with different games or by playing music on her old-fashioned lute. Melissa showed a keen interest in the music and tried to gurgle along with the sounds.

That might have been the beginning of the musical talents that emerged later on.

Closer to the departure date for returning to Taiwan, Kurt realised he could not sell the car. He decided to ship it to Taiwan, but he was worried that the humid, hot conditions for most of the year would make driving it a bit of a challenge. He tried to install an air conditioner in the car, but finally gave up. German engineering meant the vehicle had a very compact engine compartment, making it impossible to squeeze in a lumpy air-conditioning unit. The car was shipped and imported – with great difficulty – into Taiwan; the children were delighted as they loved to drive in style. Even at that young age!

All the other cars on the road at the time were made in Japan, so a Mercedes was a novelty

Later, the date of the first court hearing was finally announced.

It was fortunate that Kurt had established all the facts of the accident before and given his account in court. He now queried the odd fact that the deceased was named as the motorcycle's driver, which made little sense. The driver would have been pushed into the handle bar and broken his legs; there was no way he could have flown over the car. After a few weeks, the truth finally came out. It was revealed that the fellow with the broken leg was the driver but did not have a legal licence. He, therefore, blamed the deceased for the accident. The doctor also came clean, admitting that both had reeked of alcohol, but he did not get his fees for some weeks, so he said nothing until he received his money.

Since the civil issue had already been settled, Kurt was acquitted of any wrongdoing. He was free to go.

The prosecutor did not like the outcome and started a new action; this time it took so long that Kurt had already been transferred to a new posting in Singapore and had to deal with the court long distance. Once again, he was cleared of all charges. To make sure he had no problems when he visited Taiwan, he carried official documents of that ruling.

It was fortunate that the two children were still too young to understand what was happening and continued to enjoy their privileged lives with their friends and their families.

The children and Rebecca spent some weeks in Sydney with the grandparents while Kurt got his feet on the ground in Singapore. The house the company had leased for Kurt's predecessor was still under contract for some time and would be the new home for the family. Unfortunately, it took three months before it became vacant. Meanwhile, Kurt stayed in the Hilton Hotel on Orchard Road. Not a shabby alternative, Kurt thought. The family joined him shortly after, and Casper and Melissa became the mascots of the friendly hotel staff. The general manager, Michael Schuetzendorf, was introduced to Kurt by another Hilton manager in Taipei, James Smith, which helped him to find his way into social life by making new friends. After that, Kurt just had to stroll across the street to get to his office in Orchid Tower. That also meant he had a little more time in the morning to have breakfast with the family and plan activities for the kids. Kurt bought a small Mazda for the family, as Rebecca and the children needed to get out and explore the city, go shopping and visit friends. Kurt used a company car and driver, so that arrangement worked well.

Another German manager in the office went to the USA and sold Kurt his ski boat; he did not want to take it with him. That turned out to be an excellent investment, as it provided a badly needed break from the heavy weekly business schedule, and allowed him to spend quality time with the children. Kurt did not know how to ski, but joined a group of military guys from Australia and New Zealand who did their training in the jungle of Malaysia. Being tough, fit and young, they had the energy to enjoy the weekend sporting activities and they were kind enough to teach Kurt the basics of water skiing. Casper and Melissa did not fancy getting dragged through the water, swallowing gallons of that somewhat putrid liquid and were happy just to enjoy the ride in the fast boat. Or explore the little island the ski group used as a base for their activities. That was safe as long as they did not venture into the water. Well, it nearly was safe. Casper must have found some matches and he built a little campfire. He got that going but did not know how to contain the flames, which soon ate away at the surrounding vegetation. Luckily, the military guys had a good sense of smell and saw the smoke rising, and it took little effort to extinguish the fire before significant damage had occurred.

Kids are always hungry. Kurt had some sandwiches in a cooler, but it never seemed enough. To everybody's delight, they discovered a nearby fishing hut, standing on stilts in the water, where they bought beautiful Sri Lankan blue crabs to be put on the hot coals of the BBQ fire. It became a regular outing on Sundays, and often, there was a group of five or more ski boats with some twenty friends, locals and foreigners, joining the fun. Some groups would navigate up a small river in Malaysia for more serious skiing. Officially, it was not allowed, but that was the only place they could find calm enough waters to practice barefoot skiing. Some of Casper's friends from school, and their parents, occasionally joined in, and their friendship lasted for many years. Unfortunately, expat life does not guarantee long periods in one place. Most of the time, an overlapping stay of two or three years is typical before friends have to depart again for other assignments. That was a problematic fact to explain to Casper and Melissa whenever they again lost some friends because of their parents moving away.

Kurt had little idea about the children's activities in school. Rebecca used to be a teacher and took care of all that. Even at important events, such as sporting days, Kurt could not take time off to attend the activities. Finding companies that allowed time off for such purposes was challenging. The expat was employed to do a job and not to waste time on trivial things such as attending children's school events. That was the typical attitude and was hardly ever challenged.

Kurt's brother, Gunther, and his family visited Australia from Germany and stopped off in Singapore for a few days. The highlight of their stay was a trip to Tioman Island, off the East coast of Malaysia. That involved a car ride to Mersing, parking the car and taking a small ferry to the island's resort hotel. It was a beautiful, unspoiled beach, with clear waters sheltered from the wind and large waves. A kid's paradise to play around in, and the only danger was a better than even chance of getting sunburned. Casper had another bout of love for animals. This time for the ugliest sea-cucumbers, found in great numbers along the beach. He struck their backs, squeezed them and tried to get their attention. Nothing worked, but Casper was not easily convinced to give up on this futile exercise. Little did he realise he would eat this kind of creature years later in a special hotpot dish in a Chinese Restaurant in Hong Kong.

Another memorable trip took the family to the Club Med at Cherating Beach on the East Coast of Malaysia. A tranquil retreat, so it seemed, but exploding in a kaleidoscope of activities in the centre of the resort village. The young people acting as table waiters, room service staff and kitchen hands all had some artistic talents which went on show at various times of the day. Kurt saw little of the children, as they were keen to join the special activities available for them every fun-filled day. They did not want to return to the accommodation hut in the evening but finally dropped into their beds, very exhausted and happy.

All good things end, and the drive back to Singapore was a bit of a let down for everybody.

Casper begged them to get a dog. Kurt didn't think much of that idea, but reasoned it might help the young boy settle down and start taking responsibility. They decided to get a larger dog; they worried that Casper might injure a smaller dog, being a little clumsy and hyperactive. Secretly, Kurt had to admit that he was also warming to the idea of a dog, but he insisted it had to be a German shepherd. A breeder was found, and a young puppy was purchased at a high price. The dog looked every inch the part, with characteristic colouring, long hair, and a beautiful muzzle, and Casper became very attached to it. Finally, he had something he could hug and get a warm response such as being licked all over his face. Unfortunately, the joy did not last long. The dog seemed in pain and kept dragging one hind leg. They found out this was an outcome of in-breeding, and the conditions would only worsen with age. Kurt was furious; not because of the money they had spent but because of what the breeder did to the dogs in his care, just to make more money. Casper cried his heart out when Kurt had to take the dog back to the breeder, who reluctantly refunded the purchase money after being threatened with exposure to the breeders association in Singapore.

But what to do about Casper? Something had to be done quickly to take his mind off the departure of his beloved puppy. Kurt embarked on a kind of conjuring trick; he bought a couple of white rabbits in a pet shop to fill the void in Casper's life. They were true to their species and produced a bunch of young rabbits, which charmed the children. A square, open cage was put together in the backyard so the rabbits could enjoy the grassy areas and the kids could play with them.

One evening Kurt came home to a disaster zone. No rabbits, both kids were crying, and Rebecca was at a loss for what to do. Slowly, the story unfolded. The next-door neighbour had a dog, which seemed to have enjoyed some unexpected freedom, and took the opportunity to do some hunting in the back yard of the family's house. According to the children, all the rabbits had been killed by the dog, a traumatic experience for most humans, especially children.

A strategic decision had to be made. The next pet had to be dog-proof, easy to handle and maintain as the children spent more time in school. They bought a turtle and let it out in a little pond at the back of the house. Turtles don't run fast, but there are steady movers. A string was tied to one leg to prevent an escape, and the problem was contained. As Casper found out sometime later, a turtle is not as lovely to cuddle as rabbits are. The turtle did not like the idea and somehow lodged itself on Casper's chest, who howled in pain. A little scar formed later as a reminder of the incident.

Not long after the massacre of the rabbits, the children and Rebecca visited the grandparents in Sydney during the school holidays. Kurt had to stay behind, busy with work and the many overseas visitors who needed to be entertained when they came to Singapore. One late evening Kurt came home and had a glass of milk with a raw carrot as a night snack. Sitting outside on the veranda steps, he suddenly saw a little white snout peeking out of the drainage pipe in front of him. Quite concerned, Kurt quickly counted how many alcoholic drinks he had consumed that evening; seeing white rabbits at night could be attributed to an excessive drinking session. But, no, this one was real. It was a miraculous survivor of the tragic decimation of the white rabbit family by the neighbour's dog. It must have fled from the attacker and been hiding in the protecting drainage pipe, coming out late at night to search for food. Kurt expended a lot of patience waving the juicy carrot in front of the white snout until the rabbit finally emerged from the hideout. Then, cautiously, it would take a bite from the carrot and munch away, only to have another go a little later. It must have been starving, but it was still an effort to overcome its fear and trust this big human not to inflict any hurt. The rabbit darted back into the drainage pipe as soon as the feast was finished.

The interaction between Kurt and the rabbit became a nightly affair, and the creature was obviously not as fearful as before. But it always went back to the safety of the pipe after the consumption of one or two carrots and would not appear during the day.

On the return of the children to Singapore, they had to be coached on how to act around the rabbit so that it would not disappear again for fear of being eaten. Finally, they all agreed to let the rabbit live in the pipe and keep its existence a secret, so that the bad dog next door would never find out.

Kurt's job change necessitated moving to another house in Singapore. To move the turtle was no problem; just pull the string attached to one leg, and the turtle would appear from wherever it was hiding. It got a bit more complicated with the rabbit. It could not be left behind, as it was used to being fed every night before hiding in the pipe again. To a degree, it was a breach of trust, but Kurt had no choice. A lovely quiet evening was arranged, the most delicious-looking carrot prepared, and it didn't take long for the rabbit to appear. This time, it was grabbed by the neck, and even though it kicked a lot, it was gently put into a secure box for transportation to the new house. A nice fenced-off area was prepared for its new occupant, and life settled into a more sedate routine for the rabbit. It could hop around, enjoying the soft grass, getting fed regularly, and warming up in the sunshine.

Word must have gotten around in the dog community. A few weeks after moving to the new place, a huge dog jumped the wire fence, got hold of the rabbit and bounced back to wherever it came from. No further sighting of the rabbit or the dog was reported; it was a very sad ending to a lovely but short relationship between the children and a beautiful white rabbit.

Meanwhile, Melissa had grown into a small but very assertive young girl. Maybe she was spoiled through the constant attention from the maid, the mother, and everybody she had contact with. She was good-looking and could be very charming if she wanted something; it became almost a game to find out what that something was before the final disclosure. But even the myth about the honey bee, i.e. Melissa, did not hide the fact that she also had quite a sting when it suited her. She was very competitive and needed to be the winner at all times. Kurt was happy about that; it meant she would succeed nicely in school; she had already shown some signs in that direction. However, her sunny nature changed with playing games. She loved to play card games and pestered everybody to take part.

Unfortunately, in games, people cannot control their fortunes; luck comes into it. That means gamers can also be losers, which was never acceptable to Melissa. She had to win all the time. She would argue, she would become noisy, and she was known to cheat a little to be declared the winner. Not a nice trend for a young lady, but there was hope for the parents that this was only a passing phase.

Melissa had a lot of friends, and often, a group of girls would descend on the house to visit and play together. Most of the time, the girls and the maid would restore some order after the chaos, but one day that did not work so well. It was already bedtime for the children and the girl's room was still a total mess. Being tired, Melissa was trying to order the maid to clean up, only to be reprimanded by her mother. Again showing strong reluctance to comply with the instructions to clean up her room, Melissa displayed a fierce attitude toward everybody in the world and finally slumped into bed, totally exhausted after the long day's activity. The parents learned a vital lesson. The strong-willed daughter was not ordered to do anything but needed to be led to the task by reason and explanation. That would only work if her mind was not too tired; a slight change in routine would achieve that.

The maid was from the Philippines. She had her work cut out to keep up with the housework, do the cooking, and shop for groceries. One day, Rebecca noticed a lot of dust on the floor in the living room. The maid admitted she had not vacuumed for a few days because the vacuum cleaner seemed to have broken. For technical matters, Kurt was always ordered to investigate, although he knew nothing about electrical things, being a glorified pen pusher in the office. He could not openly admit to that and put up a show of dragging the vacuum cleaner to the terrace to clean the dust bag, before opening up whatever was to open for inspection. It was then the mystery was solved. In the middle of the dust spread out on the floor, a little snake wriggled its way towards the garden. It was less than one foot long, thin, with a tiny, ugly-looking head. His first instinct was to prevent the snake escaping. Since Kurt was unprepared for such events, he had taken no precautions or preparation. Kurt found a very effective way of slowing the snake's escape; he jumped on it with his sandal-covered feet. Then he went and grabbed a garden tool, and the snake was despatched in due course. Nobody present had a clue how to identify the creature, so Kurt put it into a glass jar and took it to the office the next day to show it to the local staff, with the same result. City people do not have that knowledge and don't want to come too close to anything that is not civilised.

Coming back to the maid. She confessed she had vacuumed the room when she saw the little snake under a piece of furniture. Being frightened, she just sucked it away, and the snake ended up in the dust bag, which she would not open for fear of being bitten. Therefore, the machine was "broken", and she would not do any more vacuuming. Now the problem was solved, and she happily attended to her duties again.

One day, the maid presented the family with the fact that she had acquired a dog. She claimed it followed her in the street a few times, and she had fed it on those occasions. Dogs love whoever feeds them, and after a lot of pleading, the family decided maid could keep the dog, to the delight of Melissa and Casper. The dog was named Bell and became a significant being in the household, even though it was very destructive, chewing on everything in sight.

One night Kurt was woken up by the maid. A terrible thing had happened to poor Bell. She was howling at a terrible pitch from somewhere in the garden. When he went to investigate, he found Bell was attached to a big male dog; it seemed they could not part company after a few moments of passion. To end their misery, Kurt took a bucket of water and cooled them down, which worked. Finally, Bell stopped howling. The big dog vanished into the night, and peace seemed to have been restored. At least for the time being.

That little encounter resulted in a litter of eight puppies, some two months later. It was a lovely sight, but having to deal with the mess of little dogs running around everywhere tested the patience of the adults in the household. Kurt was happy that the children had experienced such an event, but their looming departure from Singapore created more headaches. What to do with the dogs? The maid was willing to look after Bell, but they needed to find suitable homes for all the puppies; the alternative did not look so pleasant and was not openly discussed in front of the children.

Somehow, Rebecca persuaded several of her friends in Singapore to take a puppy or two just before the family embarked on a vessel to sail to Fremantle, WA.

Rebecca had finished her long-distance studies with a university in the USA and wanted to join the workforce again in Australia. Almost ten years of living the life of an expat stay-at-home parent had done nothing to satisfy her mental capacity, and she was looking forward to becoming a teacher again.

The family booked a small Russian cruise ship, plying the trade between Singapore and Fremantle, Western Australia (WA), to take them back home. There was no job waiting for Kurt or Rebecca. They had decided to settle back in WA after a visit to the children's grandparents in Sydney.

Sailing on the small ship could have been more comfortable. Rough seas caused seasickness to almost all the passengers in the first few days. There was plenty of food, but only a few takers. The Russian crew tried their best to keep the guests entertained. Still, there was very little interaction between passengers and crew, partially because of language problems.

On arrival at the International Terminal in Fremantle, the family met an old friend, Warwick Broomfield, who was kind enough to provide transport to the Ocean Beach Hotel, Cottesloe. After a couple of days, the excitement for the children continued as the long journey to Sydney began. The Indian Pacific train would take over three days to reach their destination, with many hours of travelling at low speed through the open countryside. However, the novelty quickly wore off, and the children needed to be kept active with games, walking through the train from the back to the front and having meals in the restaurant carriage.

Kurt did not know how to put food on the table for the family. Rebecca had no problem; she was confident she could get a teaching job anywhere in Australia.

Kurt had a couple of interviews in Sydney, but he was not happy to join the rat race of a large corporation any time soon. So he returned to Perth to find an affordable house, in the right area to provide access to good schools for the children. Rebecca would apply to the Education Department for a teaching or counselling job. Kurt was considering starting his own company, and they set some money aside as the initial investment.

The priority was to find a house. As an interim solution, they rented a place near a primary school in Jolimont for a few months, to get the children back into school. Even though they could walk independently,

Rebecca and Kurt initially accompanied them to ensure they got used to the unfamiliar environment. Melissa seemed to have no problem settling in, but Casper experienced some anxiety as his classmates were almost hostile towards him. Attending a British school in Singapore had resulted in a slight British accent; this was certainly enough for his Australian peers to pick on him. The protected life of an expat child had ended, and Casper was not mature enough to fully understand that he might also have to change his innocent attitude toward the rest of his young world.

Rebecca found a position and needed help to get back to the discipline and the long hours required to manage all the duties. It fell to Kurt to ensure the children got to school on time; then he met them again after school and supervised them until Rebecca came home. That also meant Kurt had to do housework, to ensure the uniforms got washed and ironed and that snacks were ready to be eaten after school. The evening meal was simple, but the children seemed to be happy.

To Kurt, it was indeed quite a change after working in big companies, being able to ask people to perform a specific task for him and enjoying the benefits of many helping hands. But he needed to find more time during the day to start his business. He rented a simple office, registered the company, and identified a few clients after some research. It promised to be a long road to achieving a profitable business. To ensure some cash flow, Kurt invested in a franchise business of window tinting, for which he employed three people; now he could spend more time developing contacts to further his enterprise. Western Australia was still a backwater in the freight forwarding business. Customs brokers controlled the existing business, and Kurt had difficulty getting a foot in the door. One of the main reasons was that the business community still believed that they could only trust somebody if they had stayed and worked in the same place for at least five years. The experience gained by working in other countries did not count at all.

The WA Government offered some consultancy business. There was a solid move to increase the export of perishable items, and a study was conducted to check available supplies, facilities, and requirements. Kurt looked at various commodities, which included mud crabs from the Mangrove swamps in the north, fresh Australian wildflowers, and fresh and dried South African Protea flowers from suppliers near Busselton, WA.

Each Industry had specific problems. The mud crabs had to be inspected by Quarantine before exportation, which could only be done in Perth. That meant extra transport time and additional cost. The markets in Japan needed to be reached within seventy-two hours after picking the crabs from their habitats in the Mangrove swamps. The very proud local airline was unwilling to work on the problem of space and frequency of services, as they considered themselves to be doing very well without having to work for it. Last but not least, the supply of mud crabs was complex; it was a problem getting itinerant workers to stay long enough to fulfil commitments. Many only stayed for two or three weeks, earning up to $3,500.00 per week, but left again as it was not a pleasant job stomping around the Mangrove swamps, picking up very aggressive crabs.

The WA wildflower supply was initially based on accessible roadside collections in the country. When that supply dried up, the picking of wildflowers was banned. Several farms had started production to facilitate sufficient supply. Still, they were hampered by the lack of cargo space provided by the local airline. Buyers in Europe could get flower from vast farms in Kenya within hours to be distributed all over Europe. The market, therefore, was limited for Australian producers.

South African Protea became very popular because of various factors. The political system in South Africa gave cause for concern to a lot of Caucasian people, and they wanted to migrate to Australia. The only problem was the transfer of their assets or cash, which was restricted to prevent a flight of capital from the country. Some people had a clever idea. Before migrating, they bought container loads of South African wildflower seeds, which they could ship to Australia. Once in the country, they formed interest groups to grow Protea. Many little farms got in on this promising business. Of course, the new farmers had to buy seeds from the migrants, giving them starting capital in Australia.

Kurt prepared the study and got paid, but there was no resulting business.

A friend had a small export company to send frozen prawns to overseas destinations. The procedure was quite involved, so Kurt could assist regularly and build up some good turnover. As a sideline, he also imported fresh orchids from Singapore and sold those to a few local florists. The income slowly grew, and after eighteen months, the business covered costs; but it needed more working capital to cover daily expenses until clients paid their bills.

The original agreement with Rebecca covered that situation. If the small company paid for all expenses, they could take out a mortgage on the house to provide the required working capital. The company would cover all costs involved.

Well, things sometimes work out differently than planned. Rebecca refused to countersign the mortgage through fear of losing the house. Kurt could not continue to operate without working capital and had to close the little company and look for a job. A few offers came in from the Eastern States, but the income would only be enough to cover the rent for a small bedroom and food. There was no way Kurt could support the family in that scenario.

Old European contacts introduced him to a small German forwarder in Hong Kong looking for a general manager. The package included accommodation and a reasonable salary, enabling Kurt to support his children.

By then, it was obvious that his marriage to Rebecca had been on the rocks for quite some time. The job in Hong Kong provided a compromise solution for Kurt. The children stayed with Rebecca in the family home. Kurt worked in Hong Kong, and it was no surprise when Rebecca applied for a divorce in the family court. Nothing was to be done except to ensure the children were looked after and could stay in regular contact with Kurt. There was no way that Kurt wanted arguments to drag on for years; he just signed over everything in favour of Rebecca, so the children would not have to move house and school. It also prevented any future legal arguments, but Kurt promised to keep up with his support of the children voluntarily.

Kurt had to work on a new start in life, free of all legal burdens but poor. He had two suitcases with essentials he had brought from Perth; that constituted his whole earthly wealth. Work provided the antidote to all the painful decisions Kurt had to make. Still, he managed to fly the children over to Hong Kong at least two times a year and made sure he visited Perth once every year to keep in close contact. Kids grow up quickly, making new friends, and Kurt hoped they would not be too badly affected by the split-up of their parents.

The perceived advantage of having experienced life as an expat child, albeit short, soon faded, but they succeeded in school and university.

Kurt was pleased about that and proud that they became valuable members of society.

Kurt wanted to document the story of his children in a foreign environment, living the life of expat kids. Sadly, he realised he knew very little about them and what they had experienced when they lived in Taiwan and Singapore. Because of his work commitment, there was no time for him to attend any school functions and many other activities. Companies did not appreciate their executives spending private time during working hours, and the definition of working hours was very flexible. Frequent business travels took Kurt away many times, giving him very few occasions to spend quality time with the children.

For these reasons, the story ended up being an account of what Kurt did during their time as expats and not so much about the children. Even though everything is connected somehow, maybe the children got a solid start in life by having to face adversity at an early age.

We will never know.

Author's note: I need to make a confession. The lead character Kurt is actually representing my own story. At the time of writing I found it very difficult to associate directly with that emotional time and I needed to resort to hiding behind fake names. I do apologise for trying to deceive you, the reader. Obviously the names of Rebecca and Casper are fictional as well.

The offer to become Sales Manager Western Australia for Lufthansa German Airlines sounded exciting and glamorous.

It proved to be more than that.

Outback Excursion

My first day of employment was a hectic scramble to get up early in the morning and catch a series of flights from Perth to Hamburg, Germany, via Jakarta and Frankfurt. Arriving the following morning, I just had time to check into the accommodation, have a shower and hurry to the training centre at Lufthansa to join a group of people from all over the world. The fact that I was one hour late was excused on the grounds I had travelled close to thirty hours and come straight off the last plane to join the class.

It was not my lousy travel planning which led to this somewhat tortuous start of my six-week training.

For many years the German speaking club in Perth celebrated the famous Oktoberfest in Munich with a much smaller version of this beer festival. That year I was elected to organise this event in a much bigger format looking at targeted participation of 50,000 revellers or more. All went well with the preparation, and the final event took place in the Royal Agricultural Grounds in Claremont. Tents in the centre, the giant sheep exhibition halls were decorated like a Bavarian beer cellar, TV crews ready to take shots of the action and the sideshow operators looking forward to an unseasonable boost to their income.

Steady rain turned the showground into soft mud. Most guests stayed home, and all activities concentrated on the lovely venue of the sheep hall in the showground. The brass band played catchy songs, and everybody enjoyed the scenery, including Sir Charles Court, Premier of Western Australia.

Unfortunately, as the date of this event was one day before my first official day with Lufthansa and the pre-booked training sessions in Germany, there was no way to change anything. I finally left the festivities at 2 am, only to be back at the airport at 8 am to start my journey to Germany.

Six weeks later, I had two certificates to show my test results and the first prize of one first-class flight to anywhere in the Lufthansa worldwide network. That was supposed to be the glamorous part of the job, and I was looking forward to the experience.

Back in Perth, the daily job was becoming a routine, and I was trying hard to think of something different to boost sales and income.

Our regional partner in WA was McRobertson-Miller Airlines. Because this was a mouthful, we called it simply Mickey Mouse Airline. They provided the link for our overseas passengers who had to visit mining or oil and gas operations in the North of the country.

Over a few friendly beers with the salespeople from Mickey Mouse Airlines, we came up with a grand idea of how to do something different to boost sales. Because of his employers, Scott had reason to travel to the north-west regularly and told me some stories which brought dollar signs into my eyes.

The people working in the north-west earned proportionally more money than anybody in Perth. This was justified because the work conditions were unusual. It was often hard on the body and mind and not everybody could keep up with it. A particular group of people came into our focus. Workers who serviced the heavy rail lines running from Paraburdoo to Dampier, a distance of about 300 km through harsh bushland and crossing river beds on the way. There was nothing in between except for two camps full of workers who were needed to keep up the daily maintenance of the railway line. Ore trains with 10,000 tons of ore pulled by three oversized diesel-electric locomotives would use this track daily to deliver the cargo to the port.

The point argued by Scott was that all these people earned very good money with nowhere to spend it. Every three months, they would get a long weekend in Perth. It was something of a given that they would spend a lot of money on that weekend, which would pay for a long haul trip to Paris or any other dream destination.

The idea was born. Visit the camps and show these hard-working people lovely travel movies of romantic places that would suddenly be accessible if they only diverted their hard-earned cash to our combined services.

Our planning involved flying to Paraburdoo on Mickey Mouse Airlines and hiring a car to drive along the service road, which followed the railway track to Dampier. Luck and connections were on our side; a rental car was stuck in town after repairs from an accident, and it had to be returned to Dampier. We offered to undertake the job and got free transport in return.

Our few belongings included several movies and a tiny projector, which we loaded safely into the compact car. We intended to visit two camps, about 100 km apart along the track.

The welcome in the first camp was heart-warming. The many beers on offer were not helping to cool us down in the relentless heat during the late afternoon sunshine. Our accommodation was the same as any worker in the camp enjoyed. A structure, similar to a shipping container, was set up with one or two little rooms for just one bed and a little side cabinet. A prison cell was probably more spacious and cosier.

We set up our projector outside as the camp had a central grassed area with a large white screen on one side. Obviously, that was their movie cinema, as no radio or TV was available.

The sun slowly descended, and the heat became a little more tolerable. We decided to get spruced up for the evening entertainment and headed for another, larger container, which served as a shower and ablution block. All was OK except when we discovered the place was crawling with little beetles known locally as stink beetles. They had the nasty habit of secreting a powerful, smelly liquid if touched, and although harmless, it was overwhelming to the nostrils. Our newly found friends' advice was simply to drink more beer and forget the smell.

The movies did the trick; everybody enquired how they could arrange their own travel to one of the destinations. We felt we had justified our trip and anticipated a similar reaction in the second camp. It was time to relax and join the revellers with some more beverages.

During the long hours of talking, we discovered that on the next leg of our journey, we would have to cross the Fortescue River. We knew that, but the latest news was not encouraging. The only bridge was built for the railway line; any vehicular traffic had to ford the river, and the only potential crossing place was flooded. Always the optimist, Scott pronounced that rivers would rise and fall, and we would find a way to cross. One of our inebriated drinking partners proudly mentioned that he was in charge of the big tracked machinery which they used daily to do their work. That would be capable of pulling us through the river. But he also made it quite clear that anybody touching his beloved machine would be in jeopardy of serious injuries, or worse, inflicted by him.

The following day we continued our journey, although it was harrowing. Alcohol heats the body, particularly the brain. This was not helped by the sun, high in the sky, relentlessly cooking us inside the little car, whose air-conditioning system obviously did not fulfil expectations. The unsurfaced road, used only by four-wheel vehicles, did not offer any comfort for a town car with small wheels. It took until late afternoon to reach the Fortescue River. Our friends of last night were correct; the ford next to the railway bridge was totally underwater, and we had no chance to cross the river here: Except if we had a tracked vehicle which could pull us through? A death-defying thought entered our heads; where was the tractor mentioned by our friend last night?

My ability to remember details was still reasonably intact. We found that big Caterpillar No. 9 (Cat 9) hidden in the bush, about 500 metres from the river. Ropes and chains were attached; all we had to do was start the monster up and drag our car through the river.

We searched for a key everywhere as these things usually are hidden somewhere to have it ready when needed. Not being very educated in mechanical matters, I overlooked a strange looking plastic hook-like piece of equipment under the seat. As I found out later, that was the actual key to starting the engine. The result was we were stuck. What options did we have? Going back to the first camp was out of the question; I could not handle another load of alcohol so shortly after I'd escaped those stink beetles; and going forward was temporarily out of the question until the water level in the river was lower. That could be half a day or two; who knows? We decided to wait it out, hoping that another service crew would come along the road to rescue us.

It became dark, and we scrambled through the bush to find larger branches of green foliage to make beds for the night. There was nothing to prepare; we just tried to lie down and get rid of the buzzing in our heads by sleeping it off. Unfortunately, the buzzing increased. Hot and sweaty as we were, the local band of mosquitoes found us in no time, and the buzzing outside our heads became a concert. The only satisfaction we could get was killing those monsters by the dozens, as they were big and bountiful; you could not miss any with a good swipe.

After midnight, we heard the roar of an engine and some lights striking through the bush. Four hardy travellers from the camp turned up in an impressive-looking four-wheel drive. They generously offered to pull us through the river. I am easily impressed with confidence, but there was an element of alcoholic faith I detected on the driver's breath. Therefore, I meekly suggested that they should test the waters first by driving through the ford alone, as the water level looked a bit high. They obliged laughingly and got stuck halfway through the river. Now they were slightly embarrassed, worrying we might tell the story to their mates one day. I made a deal, knowing they were cleverer than us. Surely they could drive a Cat 9 if we showed them its location? It was a trade. They should pull their own fancy vehicle through the river, then our little car, and return the Cat 9 to where it was hidden to make sure the guardian of this monster would not come after us. We, in turn, promised not to utter a word to anybody in the future, ever.

The operation took a little longer than planned, but when the first rays of the sun appeared, we were on the other side of the river, where our rescuers took off in a hurry. We had to unpack our car first and make sure the vital equipment was safe; we had almost a foot of water in the boot because of being dragged through the flooded river.

Not feeling exactly well, we drove off towards the next camp. The trouble started when our engine stopped. Maybe the water had done some damage, and we checked under the bonnet for any signs of electrical short circuits. Nothing. Scott fiddled with the carburettor to get the fuel flow going. I was totally impressed that this somehow worked so we could continue our journey. Well, for a while, at least. The engine stopped every 2 or 3 km; we had to manipulate the carburettor to get going again. Eventually, nothing worked anymore. Frustrated, we discussed how far the next camp could be. My opinion was at least 10 km; Scott was adamant it was not over 3 km. The only sign of human activities I could see was an aeroplane flying high above our heads towards the south. No use; there was no way they could spot us unless we started a huge fire. They would be 200 km away by that time, and we would be toast in these conditions.

Scott was stubborn – or thirsty. He marched off towards the next camp, only wearing shorts, a shirt and flip-flops. I didn't join him; it seemed safer to stay with the car, to make sure that at least one of us could tell the tale.

It took about two hours before a truck arrived; Scott was happily smiling from the back; after all, his estimates on the distance to the camp were far better than mine.

We got towed to the camp, set up our projection equipment for the evening's show and dropped on our bunk beds to catch up with some sleep. Meanwhile, the camp's mechanic had a good look at our car and declared that it could not be fixed for a week; he needed spare parts from Dampier. We found out later that the car had been involved in an accident near Paraburdoo, and the repairs on the fuel tank left dirt in the tank, which finally clogged up the fuel supply line.

The evening show went well, and we kept ourselves in good shape by not going overboard in our social drinking behaviour. We also needed to be nice to a particular gentleman. He had to drive to Dampier the next morning and had offered us a ride in his special vehicle. We gladly accepted the offer, but had our reservations when we realised we would be driving in a big Toyota Landcruiser, but on the railway lines. A brilliant hydraulic device would lift the vehicle up by lowering a set of railway wheels onto the rails, and off we went. Our reservations stemmed from the fact that we knew the line was busy with massive trains that could take up to 2 km to stop in case of emergencies. We were assured that we could get off when a train approached, but that was only possible at very few flat rail crossings along the ride.

Sure enough, the radio crackled halfway to Dampier, and we sped up to find the next level rail crossing to get off the line. I thought it was OK, but it was only a minute later that three huge engines pulling around 50 or more rail cars passed us on the way to Dampier. From now on, the ride was more relaxed. We just followed the train, knowing there was nothing behind us, and the mood became almost light when we saw the first outbuildings of Dampier ahead.

On the flight back to Perth, I reflected on my new-found career. Interesting, it certainly was. Glamorous was not how I would describe our recent activities in the outback. I could only hope that my dreams of being successful would lead me to live in a way more aligned with my original dreams.

By the way, I never made use of the First Class Ticket prize I received from Lufthansa. Family commitments intervened, and business never allowed a window of opportunity to take time off. Before I knew it, I had left the company to join another organisation in Taiwan.

In hindsight, it is easy to say. "Do what you can now before it is too late."

The image of an old Cuban lady smoking a cigar had stuck in my mind for many years. I had seen this picture in a coffee-table book on cigars. Apparently, the image is famous worldwide.

A Tourist in Cuba, 2006

Cigars are one of the many sins I indulge in. Years ago, I graduated my taste-buds from cigars produced in various countries like the Philippines, Indonesia, Brazil and some other manufacturing places to the unmatched quality of Cuban cigars. At least that is my opinion.

Attending a dinner in a posh hotel in Jakarta/Indonesia in previous years, we witnessed the art of a Cuban national who hand-rolled cigars. Almost green tobacco leaves came out of his little bag. Deft fingers formed cylindrical shapes, twisted the cover leave around and cut one end to finish the final product. It was a delight to taste the smoke from these fresh tobacco leaves.

The *Catador* (cigar roller/taster) did not speak any English. However, another gentleman was watching, and he could translate my questions perfectly into Spanish. It turned out this gentleman was the Cuban Ambassador to Indonesia, and we became pretty friendly, enjoying a bond through our love for cigars. His interest was more professional, trying to promote his country's famous product; mine was more the enjoyment of consumption. Therefore, it was not unusual that I bought some cigars from his duty-free stock, which he could sell at charity events. That also provided extra income for his office, as the Cuban Government seemed to have very limited funds to keep their representation open.

Many brief stories were told, and I built up the desire to visit Cuba one day to experience the country and its people. Needless to say, I also wanted to share the many brands of cigars on offer.

Over four years, different groups I associated with tried to organise a visit to Cuba, but nothing transpired. I was very disappointed and got impatient enough to determine that I would go on my own.

Gunther, my brother in Germany, decided to celebrate his 70th birthday, and his son and I plotted a surprise for that day. I would turn up unannounced, with my wife, and I invited my son, who worked in London, UK, to join us with his then-girlfriend to fly over to Hannover. Another Australian friend and his family were travelling in Europe at the time and joined us to partake in the surprise.

All went well, although my brother nearly had a heart attack seeing familiar faces from the other side of the world without prior warning.

My research over many months had given me the idea to combine this trip to Germany with a side trip to Cuba. The tourist flow from Europe to Cuba was created by operators who offered attractive packages to fly to Cuba and stay one week in a hotel of one's choice. That was my cue to take advantage of a far cheaper way to get to Cuba. My wife did not fancy the idea of following me to that unknown place and preferred to fly to Washington DC to visit her good friend for the same period. Just as well; my travels turned out to be a bit more exciting than expected.

Waiting for the departure of my flight in a little side bar at Frankfurt Airport, I got the first glimpse of what was in store. A bunch of male tourists from Austria and Germany warmed up for their own adventure by drinking lots of beer, exchanging stories of past trips to Cuba and exhibiting noisy behaviour which made me decide not to join the fun of my travelling companions.

The flight took nearly 13 hours. It was not a pleasant experience being squashed in this typical seat configuration for tourist flights and being kept awake for most of the journey by the exuberant behaviour of my travel companions. The arrival at Havana Airport just after midnight brought some relief. Most tourists were boarded onto buses to be delivered to the various hotels along a beach about 50 km from Havana City. Most Europeans were looking for some fun in the sun, to get sunburned and looked forward to the bragging sessions after returning home, talking about their wonderful holiday in Cuba.

That was not what I had in mind, and I was glad I decided to stay in the centre of Havana in a hotel offered as the refurbished 'La Inglaterra Hotel'. The journey from the airport in a dilapidated small bus was exciting enough; the dark and different-smelling countryside finally made way for what could be called a city environment. It was too dark to see anything, and my mind was too befuddled from lack of sleep; I was just happy to check into the hotel and crash out. The welcome was not exactly warm;

the hotel staff efficiently checked my credentials and told me to go up the stairs, take the second door on the left, and that is where I would find my room.

It was a room, but nothing suggested any care had been lavished on it. A bed with a worn-out cover, a small shower recess and a window facing the main town square on the other side of a road. The luxury of air conditioning was soon reduced to the convenience of drowning out the traffic noise, as the window could not be totally closed, being old and warped. The curtains were dusty, and I did not even attempt to open them for fear they might fall apart.

Too tired to care, I just wanted a shower and then try to get some sleep.

I became alert very quickly when I inspected the shower area. A simple plastic curtain prevented water from splashing into the room, but the shower head pointed directly at a power socket on the wall inside the recess. What to do? I needed a shower, but I did not want to be fried.

It is amazing what a human being can do if desperate. Maybe I should apply for the distinction of having invented a genius way of having a shower by diverting the water only onto my body without getting the electric wall outlet ignited? I am still alive, so my efforts must have been successful.

Finally, I fell into a fitful slumber for a few precious hours to prepare for the first day of adventures in Havana City.

Waking up was not a simple thing to do. Since my exciting experience in the shower, I had only a brief time to rest before the sun, and the street noise, pulled me into consciousness. My head and body were not in sync, which was not helped by the jet leg suffered because of the several hours of time difference to Germany, my starting point.

But, the true *aficionado* in search of Cuban delights will not linger, and it was time to taste the breakfast provided by the hotel. Bread, jam, coffee. I think there was some fruit, but everything looked half dead and grey.

As I had done my homework regarding the whereabouts of cigar shops, I knew the next one was only around the corner from the hotel. The La Havana Cigar Factory was one of the few 'official' cigar shops in Havana. It was strongly advised to only buy cigars in one of those places. I remember my discussions with the Cuban Ambassador in Indonesia, who gave me some background on why the Cuban Government only allowed the sale of cigars in their own controlled shops.

It happened many years ago, after the revolution in Cuba, during which Fidel Castro became the leader. The economy was in ruins, and the famous products, the Cuban cigars, were not being exported. The reason was that most of the old families who produced these cigars had fled and settled in other countries in Central America, trying to start a new business. That was a flight of capitalism from Cuba after the Communist revolution, as the two systems did not seem compatible.

It was a clever move by Fidel Castro and his advisers to invite Mr Alfred Dunhill, a famous producer and marketing guru of tobaccos and fashion articles, to give some advice to the government on how to handle the production and sales of the famous cigars. In a nutshell, it was a matter of branding and reviving the old, well-known names in the industry to get recognition. The original owners and producers had fled the country and could not sell their new products as pure Cuban cigars, although they may have started their new plantations with original Cuban tobacco plant seeds.

Cuban cigars were produced again with the old brand name, as few major distributors with the wholesale rights in their region did the marketing overseas. Prices were controlled; corruption was supposed to be eliminated in the entire chain of distribution. The scheme was very successful and was also applied to the sale of cigars to tourists coming to Cuba.

My first impression of the cigar shop was like stepping into heaven. Not that I have been there or likely will ever be, but the smell and sight of all these wonderful products packed in wooden boxes of all shapes and sizes, covered with colourful labels, were just overwhelming. I could not wait and quickly bought three boxes of cigars, which I knew from experience were first class.

The staff wrote an invoice by hand; computers were nowhere in sight. I got an official-looking copy with the details of my purchase handwritten on blue and grey-coloured paper. It was emphasised that I would need this important document if I wanted to export those cigar boxes when leaving the country. OK, I thought, other countries, other habits. With paying, I realised it was another country, but it seemed the same patterns existed here as in Frankfurt or Dubai Duty-Free shops. The cigars were priced exactly the same as in those places. Whatever happened to a free economy? Shouldn't the products be much cheaper in the country where they were produced?

Never mind, depending on one's point of view, it was still a bargain.

Not long after, I almost regretted the purchase. Walking along the streets, going into small alleys in the old part of the city, I was often accosted by characters who offered me very good-looking and good smelling cigars. They had no *banderols*, no brand name, but represented part of the black market, which existed everywhere in the country. One-third of the price of a comparable cigar from the shop; the same quality, as far as I could make out. I bought a few of those to have my little smoke-in whenever I found a cosy place in the city.

The old town has plenty of those places. Almost on every street corner, you can find a little bar, have a strong Mojito and light up your own cigar with everybody's approval. The best part was that nearly every bar had a live band with four to seven members playing tantalising music, making the entire atmosphere, smoke and all, a very intimate experience. In defence of the establishments, I must mention that all windows and doors are always open. The climate is accommodating enough to allow that, and the music drifting out entertains the locals who hang around outside to enjoy the tunes for free.

The lack of sleep caught up with me. Maybe it was partially because of the Mojitos and cigars I had; whatever, I needed an afternoon nap.

My impression of the accommodation had not improved, but who cares when you are dead on your feet?

It was late afternoon when I was woken by a loud commotion. Peering through the dusty curtains, I saw a large group of men in the open space opposite the hotel. They were arguing noisily, swinging their arms wildly; I waited to see the first punches being thrown. What was I witnessing: a new revolution starting?

The strange thing was watching a group of three police officers standing in a corner and enjoying what they saw, but not taking any action. On deciding I could be enticed to some food, maybe another cigar and definitely another Mojito, I descended to the hotel's reception and enquired about the happenings outside. That was almost the only time I noticed a sign of a smile on the face of the otherwise very sombre staff. "No, everybody is happy; Cuba loves their baseball games, and the men outside were excited about the results their favourite teams had achieved."

That was a relief, but I decided I would never go to a live baseball game with that lot; surely they would get out of hand being so close to the action?

It was getting darker, and I made my way through old cobbled streets towards the town centre. I was assured all was very safe as the police I had seen were the Tourist Police, whose task was to ensure that no foreigner would come to harm. Later I suspected they also made sure that the locals did not get too friendly with foreigners, as the government was still wary about tourists coming into the country but desperately needed the foreign exchange.

The buildings on each side looked like they would not make the next decade. At one place, a creaky wooden door opening gave a glimpse of the inner courtyard. Actually, it looked odd, and it became obvious that the courtyard used to be part of a house which had collapsed, leaving only some surrounding walls standing. An old heap of a car wreck was abandoned inside, with nothing much else to see. What a surprise to see three or four young ladies stepping out of the door into the street. All dressed in white dresses or pant suits, immaculately clean and groomed. All laughs and giggles, and even humming a cheerful song on their way to whatever place they intended to meet their friends.

It was not my day to check out the nightlife of Havana; I gobbled down the local standard food of ancient chicken, long dead, and the almost compulsory black beans, which needed to be cooked for hours to make them fit for human consumption. Thanks to Mojitos, all was well after, and I even ventured to have another cigar before attempting to get a full night's rest back in the hotel.

The dismal breakfast did not improve my sense of well-being, so a walk into the old town was required, where I surely could find a place for lunch, Mojitos and cigars?

Walking a short distance past the identical wrecked dwellings of yesterday, I was pleased when I saw that several historic buildings near the seaside had been restored almost to their former glory. But, curious as I am, I checked out some bronze plaques attached to the wall. Then, finally, I saw a note that all the funding for the restoration work was donated by one of several European countries to help preserve some of the history and beauty of old Havana.

The tourists began to arrive in the city by bus from their modern hotels along the beaches. Slurping a coffee, I sat in a little place in the dark interior and watched the sorry sight file past. It was like watching a horde of mixed farm animals being shepherded by tour guides. There is something about a group of tourists from different countries, but they have a lot in common; they plunge into the little streets, follow the leader to the next tourist attraction, which is on the official list of 'must do' and carry on from there. Cameras are clicking, loud voices call out, and the physical appearance of each one could bring tears of laughter or disgust to one's eyes.

Some men dressed up in whites and a Panama hat, invoking visions of Hemingway doing his bit in the city. Others did not even try to hide their enormous bellies in far too small pants, or wore tiny shorts which showed off their white legs, not touched by any sun yet. I will not even try to comment on the lady's attire, as I could easily be accused of being rude, and it would mostly just be total ignorance on my part; I do not know what the appropriate clothing should be.

To hide my amusement, I smoked another cigar so I could always claim my teary eyes resulted from my cigar fumes.

I thanked good fortune that most tourists come to Cuba to soak up the sun by staying along the beaches in faraway hotels, which meant they had to leave the city by around 4 pm, and I could claim the place back to roam around without having to sidestep another stampede of anxious tourists worried they may miss out on another photo opportunity.

Life was not bad in the quiet surroundings, with history creeping into my thoughts, fuelled by Mojitos and cigars. Havana in the early 20th century must have been quite a place to enjoy.

One should never forget to get some exercise when indulging in a sinful lifestyle, even if it is just for a week. So I decided to go for a long walk, and it was at the far end of the town that I noticed a fairly decent little hotel with a bar inside. I noted it down for exploration for another day and carried on enjoying the scenery of this ageing city.

I was only a short distance away from that hotel when a youngish-looking gentleman dressed in a suit greeted me in halting English. The usual "hello, what is your name, where are you from?" I mentioned I am from Germany, which prompted him to announce that he had a German fiancée back in Germany. He said his intention was to visit her as soon as possible.

I am not easily sucked into strange schemes that intend to open my purse to support strangers. Still, he looked decent and better off than most of his compatriots and the statement that he worked in the hotel I just had discovered made it more plausible; this is where he had seen me first. We decided to go for a drink as it was his time off. He loosened his tie around the neck, and a pub crawl started, taking in at least six to seven establishments. Everywhere my new-found friend Eduardo was greeted like a well-known person; I was introduced, and many Mojitos were consumed. At one stage, I asked Eduardo if the famous Buena Vista Club still existed. Back in Perth, I had been to a performance of this group with the same name, and at least one or two of them were still the original members, and it really got me ticking. Eduardo said if I was interested, he would take me to a place that evening. How could I say no to such an excellent offer?

Not realising what was coming, I followed Eduardo, taking a taxi ride to a destination about 40 minutes away. We got out, and he told the driver to wait, as taxis were difficult to find. Eduardo knocked on a door; nothing happened. He shouted, yelled and finally the door opened, and a face of an elderly lady appeared. She obviously knew him, and a rapid discussion in Spanish took place. The door closed again, and Eduardo guided me across the road to another house and introduced me to his friends there, who were busy with some card game and drinking Rum. No one spoke English, so I sat and watched while Eduardo returned to the house opposite.

It must have been at least 50 minutes before his return. On his arm was an attractive, youngish lady with too much make-up, who was introduced as Eduardo's girlfriend. I did not ask what was happening to the fiancée in Germany; that was none of my business.

The taxi took us back into town, and we ended up in a night club which was much more modern compared to what I expected from the Buena Vista Club. More friends of Eduardo were already assembled; a lively band soon made me forget the stylish surroundings, and I settled into a routine of sucking my cigar and drinking more Mojitos. One of Eduardo's friends came from Mexico and spoke good English. We tried to communicate over the music's din, but what was said did not matter. Maybe the electrifying atmosphere of the music got everybody under its spell. All the male patrons seemed to be having a great time with their mates; the females could not sit still and moved to the rhythm, standing right next to their table, totally absorbed in whatever they thought they were experiencing.

With all the hospitality experienced, I had to show my appreciation and invited the lot for a round of drinks. When it came to paying, I realised it was more expensive than expected, and since I did not have enough cash, I produced my credit card. No problem there, but I never feel good about using it in a strange place. My friend Eduardo was very concerned about my well-being and even made sure I was not robbed by the washroom attendant and was standing outside the cubicle whenever I had to visit.

It was time to get back to the hotel in the very early hours. Eduardo had promised to take me to another cigar shop the next day, as he had some contacts that could get me a price reduction of up to 60 per cent. Naturally, I was keen to find out what they had, and we agreed to meet the following day at the hotel. A slight complication occurred when boarding the taxi at the club. I realised I had lost my little wallet with the credit card. Panic set in, and a frantic search found nothing left inside the club. I was just about the resign myself to the fact that I had been robbed when a guy turned up with my wallet, everything safely inside. He was happy to return it to me for a small finder's fee of Euro 20.00. In the local currency, it must have been a month's salary, but what choice did I have? I was happy to have my wallet back as my holiday could have ended suddenly without it.

I don't think I noticed the very basic surroundings of my accommodation when I fell into bed that night to catch up with some hard-earned rest.

Shopping is not my usual thing to do. The exception is when my attention was concentrated on a whole batch of quality cigars that were supposed to be extremely cheap compared to normal standards.

That got me out of bed the following morning, even though my head was slightly numb after the previous night partying around town into the wee hours of the morning. Eduardo arrived at my hotel on time as promised. A clapped-out taxi of no particular pedigree transported us to a very run-down part of town, which took about 30 minutes. When I asked Eduardo why the cigar shop was in such an area, he told me we needed to pick up his driver and a private car, as the contact in the cigar shop did not like people turning up in taxis. What could I say to that? Another round of shouting and knocking on doors produced a young, blond fellow, introduced as Eduardo's driver. He even had a car which, at a push, might resemble an old Volkswagen Golf that had experienced significant makeovers in the past years. We scrambled into the small vehicle and went directly to a petrol station nearby to fill up the tank, which appeared to be empty. I obliged and paid the bill to contribute to the day's activity.

After another 30 minutes drive back to town, we ended up in a small back lane in the city's centre. After a short reconnaissance, Eduardo invited me to come through the back door, and I was astonished to see a big store with several customers buying cigars and smoking paraphernalia. I was taken through an empty office into the walk-in humidor, which had an impressive display of cigars in boxes of twenty-five sticks. Eduardo explained that the office normally would be occupied by his friend, who used to be a General in the Cuban Army before taking up this position in the cigar shop on retirement. OK, it was obvious that the General did not want to be mixing with a foreigner for whatever reason. Eduardo showed me a lot of cigars in different sizes and various well-known brand names, each one more tempting than the others. Luckily I still had some brain power left after the night before and remembered that I would need an official invoice when buying cigars in Cuba, which were part of the government regulatory requirements to prevent smuggling. Eduardo assured me there would be no problem. He suggested I point out which cigars I would like; we could then proceed to lunch, and the cigars would be delivered to me with the invoice. Since I was not asked to pay then and there, I agreed.

The driver took us to a large private house where lunch was supposed to be served. Naturally, I was concerned as the government did not allow such private business at that time. Still, when Eduardo assured me that the house belonged to his friend, the General, I did not feel any need to panic.

We were greeted by a smart-looking elderly gentleman who turned out to be the brother of the General. Ex-Army Security, if I remember the introduction correctly. He acted as the *maître d'*, seated us at a family dining table in the room and took our order for food and beer. That done, we received some more guests. A well-groomed plump lady and her little son of about ten years old joined us for lunch. I suspected they were close relatives of Eduardo.

The food was far better than anything in the local restaurants; some great seafood and vegetables found their way to the table. Connections obviously helped to obtain such ingredients.

After a couple of beers, I relaxed and started feeling good. The awakening came when the driver turned up and handed me a plastic bag with four boxes of cigars which I must have indicated earlier in the shop. The asking price for the cigars was really very little, but the snag was that he did not bring me the official invoice. What to do? Do not pay until the invoice is presented or pay and hope that the promise of getting me that piece of paper would be kept? By that time, I was pretty awake and sober. I looked at the driver closely and realised he looked incredibly fit. Somehow I had visions of him fighting in the deep jungle of Africa during the insurgency in Angola, which was supported by Cuba. He most likely was the bodyguard of Eduardo, I had no doubt.

My conscience told me not to agree to blackmail, but I felt vulnerable and slightly intimidated. The brain said that paying a few dollars for cigars was worthwhile considering the possibility of ending up in hospital needing major constructive surgery on my face. My brain won; I paid and politely reminded Eduardo of his promise to give me an official invoice.

The lunch was paid for by me as well. Not too cheap, but far better than I could get anywhere in town. No complaint. Eduardo and the driver took me back to the hotel, and we agreed he would come the following week to deliver the invoice before I departed Cuba. I also had to pay more to the driver as he had acted as a taxi and needed some income.

After the day's excitement, I admired my purchases and lit one cigar to perform a tasting session. It was a genuine product, but you never know until you tried a second cigar from a fresh box to confirm; the quality was definitely good. The next little mental exercise was to work out how to import those cigars into Australia after my return. Regulations allowed me to import 25 cigars as a duty-free concession. Still, on any excess, I would have to pay customs duty. Luckily my mathematical genius gave me a quick answer to my calculations. Even after paying duty in Australia, the purchase would be a reasonable bargain considering the low price I paid for the goods.

Having satisfied my cigar shopping urges, I decided to play tourist to see the famous tobacco-growing area of Pinar del Rio. The hotel tourist desk suggested a bus tour that would also visit another renowned tourist site along the route, described as a beautiful and unique cave.

Saturday morning, a small group of tourists met outside the hotel and boarded a bus under the guidance of a female tour guide. She could speak Spanish, English and German. Looking well-groomed and a little exotic, she must have made quite an impression on four fellow Germans who seemed to have an enjoyable time talking to her.

Tobacco growing is quite an art. The soil, climate and the added flavours are increased by fermenting the leaves for up to three years in wooden boxes after harvesting. No fertiliser or pesticides are ever used, and the land will rest for up to five years in between crops to recuperate.

The actual manufacturing of the cigars is fascinating. All the tobacco in a good Cuban cigar comes from the same field. Smaller leaves are used for the filler; a wrapper is slightly bigger and holds the filler together. The finished cigar will be checked manually for any uneven or blocked spots before being put into a wooden form, checking on the thickness and length. After cutting it to the correct length, one more process is required. The cover leaf, the prime leaf on the plant, is carefully prepared by cutting out the veins to get a clean-looking, spotless cover wrapped around the cigar to make it look perfect. All that is done by hand to qualify as 'hand-rolled'.

I was taken in by the expertise of these men and women, by the wonderful smell of fermenting tobacco and the aroma of the smoke coming from consuming these cigars.

The next stop was the well-advertised cave. Several buses had already arrived, and our tour guide asked us to wait inside the bus until some other groups had left. That clearly showed the cave was tiny and could only accommodate a few people at any one time.

We used the time to question the Cuban tour guide on her vision of life in Cuba. She was very positive, almost enthusiastic. "Simple, yes, but great spirits, community and leadership." I could almost hear the brainwashing which must have taken place before she could qualify for such a position, in constant contact with foreigners. Sure enough, my German compatriots brought up the question about Fidel Castro. There was an obvious fascination that nobody seemed to know where Fidel Castro actually resided. Many reports mentioned he had up to 18 different properties, which was not exactly in line with the image of the revolutionary socialist running the country.

The well-trained tour guide got a bit aggravated and explained that Fidel was under constant death threats; the American CIA had tried to assassinate him before and had not given up on that. Therefore Fidel had to move regularly from one place to the other to stay safe. But, as always in politics, some facts mixed with folklore will have the desired effect, and our tourist group could not argue with that.

I cannot remember anything about the cave. Clearly, it was not worthwhile to stop there. Still, Cuba did not have many tourist destinations, and anything would have to do. At the end of the day, I was not happy, except for the fascinating visit to the cigar plant. There had to be more to see and experience. I was determined to learn more about this fascinating country and its friendly people.

In the previous year, I had met two gentlemen who travelled around Australia to promote Havana Club Rum from Cuba. At a function in our local Cigar Lounge, we were given the opportunity to taste a variety of Havana Club Rums at various stages of maturity. Obviously, we smoked our cigars to enjoy with the straight rum or the expertly mixed Mojitos. The recipe for that famous Cuban drink can be varied, but the simplest version is that it must have plenty of rum, a good portion of sugar, a bunch of fresh mint leaves, lime juice and club soda. Then, depending on your urgency to get inebriated, you replace the quantities of soda with rum.

My Spanish speaking skills are non-existent, and therefore I have difficulty remembering and pronouncing the names of these Cuban gentlemen. I have to live with "the friendly face but no name" approach. They spoke good English, and as they invited any visitor to Cuba to look them up, I made an appointment a few weeks before my arrival in Havana to meet them to arrange a tour of the Havana Rum Museum.

A short taxi ride later, I was dropped in front of a historic building in the old part of town. I was greeted by the two gentlemen whose names I could not remember and taken on a private tour through the museum, which showed the history of the rum industry in Cuba. They also produced rum on the premises and encouraged visitors to taste one of the most famous products of their country. A small lunch was served, and during the conversation, my hosts suggested we meet again in the evening for dinner and a show in the Hotel Nacional de Cuba, which was close to the waterfront. I gratefully accepted the invitation, not knowing what was in store for me.

The same afternoon I had the chance to meet the representative of our company in Havana. He was a nice, gentle man, soft-spoken, with a warm smile; he gave me a quick overview of the limited business in Cuba. The American embargo and the severe restrictions imposed on trade gave little opportunity to create a profitable business. His task was mainly to hold up the flag of the company and advice on some issues regarding exports and imports. The office was actually a branch of the Spanish organisation, as Spain still maintained its traditional business relations with Cuba, including the importation of cigars and rum. One has to remember that Cuba was a colony of Spain from 1492 to 1898. During this time, sugar and tobacco farming created lucrative income for Spain. Therefore, it is no surprise that there are still many connections to Cuba that will not heed the USA's embargo.

We finished our friendly discussions over a beer in a local street café and parted with regret that our relationship would be difficult to develop further because of the geographical hurdles imposed by our respective countries of abode.

It was time to get ready for dinner with the Havana Club people. There was no dress requirement as it seems that hardly anybody ever wore a suit. Smart casual was the only outfit I had on this trip, and that would have to do.

On arrival at the Hotel Nacional de Cuba, my first impression was to acknowledge that this was an actual hotel compared to where I was staying. A large entrance hall with the check-in lobby on the side and many glass doors leading to various corridors and to the outdoor garden restaurant was pretty impressive, considering that everything else I have seen in Havana was run down and in desperate need of repair. The name of the hotel gave a last clue. Hotel Nacional de Cuba was the officially sanctioned government hotel to be used as a showpiece for any visiting foreign diplomats or dignitaries. Even though I do not fall into one of those categories, I was happy to be invited to such a place and eagerly made enquiries to find out where I could locate my host in the garden restaurant. The climate made the dinner even more pleasant. Great food from a huge buffet, a BBQ producing delicious seafood, and my taste buds were stimulated even more with the inevitable Havana Club rum.

Maybe it was just as well that we had to finish our meal to proceed to the theatre located inside the hotel. Otherwise, I may have indulged in more rum than I could handle.

A milling crowd pushed through large doors into a venue with comfortable seating arrangements and a large stage in front. It was the Club Parisienne. Friendly ushers in fancy costumes showed us to the pre-booked seats, and another drink was offered. Somehow this felt very familiar, and I remembered my visit to the Lido in Paris some years ago, where one of the biggest variety shows in Europe was performed.

The music started, and the curtains rose slowly to reveal a large assembly of singers and dancers who swirled around the stage in dazzling and sometimes revealing attire. The show went on for nearly two hours, with a variety of songs and dances with varying rhythms and ever-changing costumes. I certainly did not expect such an excellent performance, equalling anything I had seen before in various places in Europe. What a sight, what music! The Moulin Rouge-style production featured performers who held the audience spell-bound, and their talents would have given great pleasure and enjoyment to any heterosexual or gay person in the world. After two hours, it became a big blur of colours, and I was happy to head back to my hotel and my noisy but soothing air conditioners to get a good sleep.

My earlier experience joining a tourist group on an organised bus trip to the tobacco-growing area near Havana was not what I had expected or liked. So I decided to have another excursion, but this time organised by me and only for me.

There was a tour desk of sorts in the hotel where government-employed people advised tourists on what to do while monitoring their activities. Apparently, the Cuban Government needed the foreigner's money but did not like the western influence which came along with that. Surprisingly, they also offered cars for rent, and that was exactly what I was looking for. A private company or person could not import a vehicle, even if they could pay the exorbitant price for foreign exchange certificates. However, the rental was quite reasonable, and I got a tiny tin box with wheels and a small engine to keep me mobile. Never mind, it was just for the day to have a little country run.

The simple tourist map I got sufficed to identify the general direction I had to take out of the city to join the *autopista*, which could be considered a highway connecting the larger cities on the island. I intended to just drive out of Havana for some distance and then try to get on to more minor country roads to see how the people in the villages lived and worked. After all, I was not coming to Cuba just to drink rum and smoke cigars; I wanted to educate myself about the local society and understand why Cuba featured highly as a favourite destination in the last century. At least that was my intention.

It was evident that Havana did not have a functioning public transport system. Some large buses plied the city but looked like converted horse floats. Packed with people, they noisily rambled through town, blowing black smoke out of their exhaust system. Infrequent schedules, lack of capacity and presumably cost forced many people to stand on the roadside trying to hitch-hike a ride from other vehicles. It is a fact that the government actually encouraged drivers to pick up stranded people to eliminate some of the transportation problems in the country and even the cities.

I negotiated the roads out of Havana, and I joined the *autopista*, following the route taken by the bus on my previous excursion. I had no idea where to go.

The principle of the *autopista* was like Germany's *autobahn*, which is a wide, dual carriage road with no crossroads slowing down traffic.

The reality was that Cuba did not have the money to do it right; there were no bridges across the highway, and every crossroad was level, which meant the whole idea of a highway without other traffic crossing was not workable. There were no fences alongside the highway stopping cows, goats and dogs from straying across anywhere and anytime. That took care of any notion of speeding in my little contraption. On every main crossing, many people milled around, almost jumping onto the road when another vehicle approached. I could not believe the number of people taking pot luck to get from A to B by hoping to find a driver to take them along. Observing how this was done, I realised that every empty car or truck stopped, people talked to the driver about where they wanted to go, and if the destination matched, they hopped in.

Something nudged me, and I thought, "Let's see what is happening". I decided to stop at another cluster of people and discover how this would develop. The first person to win the race to my car was a young lady with a chocolate complexion who spoke very limited English. Asking me where I was heading did not help since I did not know. Instead, I tried to find out where she was going, which didn't help either because I did not know any places around.

Meanwhile, a cute little girl dressed up like a doll and a rather large, chestnut-skinned lady approached. As it turned out, the grandmother was taking her daughter and granddaughter to a family gathering in a nearby village. I told them to hop into the car, and I would take them there if they gave me directions. Big Grandma was placed in the passenger seat, and the daughter and granddaughter struggled onto the back seat.

"Nearby" is an expression which apparently has many interpretations. In this instance, our journey took us some further distance on the highway before I was directed to turn left, right, and left again, by which time I was truly lost.

The road got smaller and rougher, and repairs were urgently needed to fill the many potholes. Communication was very limited, but we arrived wherever the family wanted us to be. They piled out of the car once we entered a small courtyard belonging to a simple house in a village. I got the feeling I had been adopted as the driver for the day as there was a quick command *"un momento"* from Grandmother indicating they would not stay long. They disappeared inside the house, and it was only a short time later that some singing and shouting took place. I could not figure out if it was a birthday party or a funeral, but it took much longer than I expected. Well, since I did not waste my time as a Boy Scout years ago, I was always well prepared. This time with a cigar, just the right medicine for me to blend in and fight the boredom of the wait.

A young fellow appeared on his own, and he tried to practise his English with me. I could not figure out much, but by then, my passengers appeared, chatting away happily. A group of younger people joined them in what I presumed to be a teary farewell. Then I was asked if I could stop off in the next village to drop off a passenger. Why not, since I had nothing else to do.

I got a bit worried when seven people tried to climb into my little car. They did not mind close contact. Grandmother was again in the front passenger seat, and the rest of the group somehow packed themselves at the back with the little girl posing on top of the bundle. Comfort was not in my mind but the worry of hitting another pothole in the road with the total weight of the load in my car. To my relief, it was only 30 km to the next village. The rest of the group unpeeled themselves from their tangle in the back, and an emotional farewell took place. I had noticed before that hugging and kissing was the thing to do. Very warm and passionate, except that it was not real kissing but making a lot of kissing noise when hugging cheek to cheek. The more kissing noise and longer the hug must have showed the amount of love they felt for each other.

Another drive into the unknown followed. I had to stop twice in a little village because Grandmother was unsure where to go. It seems her mother lived in this village, but the address was not precise. We always think it is no problem, just pick up the telephone and ask? Well, not in Cuba, as I have witnessed before in Havana. Here we were on some little village road, and Grandmother was shouting over fences and walls to find out where her mother was living. Just as well, the village was not that big; the commotion in a small cottage revealed some relatives and Grandmother's mother being totally overwhelmed with the unexpected visit. Obviously, the little girl had never met her Great-grandmother before, and the kissing session seemed to go on forever.

It was decided to prepare a meal from black beans and a little chicken quickly. That seemed to be the staple Cuban diet from what I observed.

Except there are not too many chickens affordable to the people, and I was greatly embarrassed when I was invited to join the meal. I had no choice, as I was worried about offending the host, but contributed a little by crossing the road to a little corner shed where an enterprising young man sold cans of Coca-Cola. Don't ask me how he got hold of that commodity in Cuba but it was the right gift to the family. There would have been no way they could afford such luxury, but for me, it was relatively little money.

During the meal, I ensured I had only one small piece of chicken on my plate. I filled up with rice, had one Coke and proceeded to the front door, where I had spotted a couple of comfortable reclining chairs. The family had so much to talk about; they most likely had not seen each other for several months, if not years. I left them to it and lit a cigar to watch the slow world go by. Some curious looks from people walking past were expected as a foreigner was undoubtedly not the most common sight in the village. But nobody approached me to say hello; the officially recommended invisible barrier between Cubans and strangers was observed, as if contact with a foreigner could corrupt their socialistic way of life.

It was not long before an older man joined me from the house. I do not know who he was or what he was doing there. The only thing in common was we both obviously enjoyed our cigar, the occasional little smile on our faces our total communication. It was a very comfortable experience for me, and I did not mind that the ladies in the house kept talking as if they wished that day would never end.

Grandmother asked me to drive them to one more destination, and as a token of thank you, she promised to show me the most lovely tourist place in Cuba after that. How could I tell them I was depending on the family to show me the way back to Havana? I kept that quiet and cheerily offered to drive them to the next place, some distance away. The destination turned out to be the house of Grandmother's brother. On arrival, they were greeted with the now-familiar hugs and kisses, but only the brother's wife and a son of around 14 years of age – who spoke excellent English – were at home. Finally, I could get a bit more information about the society and way of life in Cuba.

His father was still at work at a resort nearby. That was actually the famous tourist place I had been promised as a reward for playing taxi driver all day. It was decided that we would go there, have a look around and by that time, the father would finish his shift and come home with us for a coffee and chat.

When we arrived at the resort, we were greeted by this big, solid man in uniform with a handgun strapped to his belt and a walkie-talkie in his hand, blaring away. The father was employed as a security guard in the resort to protect whatever. He also had a good command of English, and we had a quick walk through a small forest with rather dry and sick-looking trees until we arrived at the major attraction. It was a waterfall, supposed to be the highest waterfall in Cuba, maybe some 70 metres from top to bottom. The only problem was that no water fell over the edge, and the waterfall was totally dry. It was the driest month of the year, with no rain for many weeks and the whole tourist attraction became a rather sorry sight to witness.

Some more rapid discussion on the walkie-talkie followed. A tour bus with a group of Chinese tourists had arrived and had to be taken care of before the father finally could sign off duty by transferring his gun and walkie-talkie to his rostered colleague.

The following hour was a pleasant experience in Grandmother's brother's house. Strong Cuban coffee was brewed, and I could chat in English with the brother and his son and gleaned a little family background history. The ladies talked amicably in Spanish about whatever they had to say to each other. Grandmother's brother used to be in the army and spent time in Angola during the various military actions supported by the Cuban Government. On his return, he was lucky to find this job as a guard in the tourist resort, making what seemed to be a decent living considering local circumstances.

I had to remind Grandmother it was getting late, and I did not fancy driving back to Havana in darkness. Our little group was hushed on the way back, too many impressions and news to be processed, I presume. I was directed to drop off the daughter and the little girl at one place and took Big Mama to her street. The directions on how to get back to my hotel were vague; all I knew was I had to go through a tunnel just a few streets away. No problem to find that, but coming out the other end, I could see only a few lights in the road and recognised nothing. When I finally figured out that the tunnel was a shortcut under a river which ended up in the harbour, I had some idea where to go. Just following the waterside, I approached the old part of Havana I had visited several times on foot. A couple more turns, and I was pleased to see the hotel in front of me. I was tired and not very hungry. After a cold beer, all I needed was a bed to sleep in. It had been a long day with incredibly novel experiences compared to the typical tourist trap.

My time in Havana was nearly over. Another couple of days to soak in the atmosphere, enjoy a few more cigars and slowly wean me off the Mojitos. Back home, I would not need the potent rum concoction to make my surroundings look like paradise.

However, there was one important task to be completed before I left. I had four boxes of cigars I had bought from Eduardo and still had not received the promised official invoice, so I phoned him to arrange a meeting in the nearby hotel where he claimed to work.

I arrived a little earlier than the time agreed and enquired about Eduardo at the reception; it soon became clear that nobody knew him or that he was employed by the hotel. This actually did not surprise me as Eduardo had displayed a lot of charm and made lots of efforts to get me to buy cigars from his friend by showing me around town. He introduced me to many people while trying to impress me, but all I could see was that he displayed all the signs of a clever conman, and I confirmed that later when I had the expenses to prove it. I did not get into this position because I am totally naïve. I would describe it more as being curious about how the local system works, and to find the answer, you may have to take a few small financial risks.

Eduardo finally arrived with another gentleman claiming to be his cousin. But by this time, I was dubious about any claims made by Eduardo and listened to him with suspicion. This cousin claimed to have access to many comfortable houses in Cuba which, at one stage, had been used by Fidel Castro as hideouts whenever he thought the CIA was trying to assassinate him. I remembered the story being told by the tour guide on my brief excursion to the countryside, but I could not clearly remember whether I may have mentioned this discussion to Eduardo at an early stage. In case of doubt, assume you are right, I reminded myself.

Soon the reason for putting me in the picture fell into place. They offered me a deal in which they promised me a healthy commission for introducing overseas friends and contacts and persuaded them to have a luxurious holiday in Cuba staying in one of those houses. Final details would be given once I had a chance to investigate what interest there may be from intended travellers to Cuba. It all sounded very impressive, and some years earlier, I would have swallowed this story, hook, line, and sinker but not this time – I was aware.

I made some promises to look into this exciting offer. Meanwhile, it was time for Eduardo to produce the invoice, which was still outstanding. The ultimate promise was that he would deliver this piece of paper in the afternoon to my hotel. Almost friendly handshakes finished the meeting, and I needed to go for a walk to clear my head and simmer down my temper.

Always a sceptic, I was astonished when I had a call from Eduardo in the afternoon. We met in the lobby, and he showed me an official invoice for the boxes of cigars I had bought. Before handing over this document, he mentioned that getting someone to provide this invoice had cost him money. Then, just as I had suspected, the final spin. To end the show, I produced Euro 20.00 and got my invoice, which I needed to prove that I did not buy these cigars illegally.

It was time to pack my few belongings and the boxes of cigars I had acquired. The week had been a great experience, but to prevent me from becoming an alcoholic, it was time to leave this island.

Early next morning, the ride to the airport was long and tiring. Having to endure another 13 hours sitting in a metal tube flying across the Atlantic did not inspire me to have happy thoughts. The check-in was working well; I got into the departure hall to have a cool beer and mentally switch off while waiting for the flight to depart. It took three calls over the public address system before I recognised my name. Reluctantly I went back to the customs exit port to report to one official-looking lady who asked me if the suitcase in front of her was actually mine. After confirming my ownership, the lady asked me to open the suitcase for inspection. Naturally, she found several cigar boxes, which she carefully separated into two lots. She requested to be shown the official purchasing invoice, which I was happy to comply with. One lovely colourful invoice from the first shop I visited after my arrival; a second invoice for the lot I bought through the introduction of Eduardo.

At this stage, a younger and friendly Customs Officer approached and took over the proceedings. We had a friendly discussion, and he explained what was happening.

All cigar boxes bought in Cuba in an officially approved shop would have a heliograph glued to the box, which would show up when the suitcase is being put through the X-ray after checking in. Unfortunately, four of my boxes did not have this heliograph. When I showed him the invoice from Eduardo, the officer showed me a little machine in the corner with a blue light shining in front. I had seen something like that in a bank in Asia when they screened bank notes to find counterfeits. The invoices were examined under this blue light, and one showed a watermark embedded in the invoice form, which one could not see with a naked eye.

The second invoice did not show such a watermark; it was a fake document produced with the help of a colour photocopy machine, but all other details were correct. The officer got my little story of the naïve tourist who obviously got conned by a clever local person; he must have heard that many times before. An official form was filled in with the details of the illegal cigar boxes. I was informed that I would not get fined, but they would have to confiscate the cigars; the ones covered by the correct invoice were free to go. Then I got a copy of the confiscation certificate, all very neat and tidy. I was very impressed by the efficiency of the system and the way the friendly officer handled the whole procedure.

It was not long before our flight was called for boarding.

I did some calculations. On the downside, my suitcase was lighter now, minus some boxes of cigars. I had a certificate proving I had been caught with contraband goods, and I had paid a fair amount of money in this total transaction.

On the upside, I did not have to go to prison; I may even have helped some poor Cuban with a few extra Euros, although I thought the corrupt General and his friends did not need the extra cash. But, on the other hand, I am sure they siphoned off enough from the public for personal gains; power translates into money everywhere.

Another, more pleasant surprise waited for me after arriving in Germany. Unpacking my suitcase, I found one additional box of cigars which the Customs Officer had actually written up as contraband. That was a nice gesture on his part; I just hope he did not get into trouble for his consideration.

Looking back, I think many things are wrong with how Cuba has been treated. Exploited for hundreds of years by Spain, later dominated by powerful moneymen from the USA until President Batista's corrupt Cuban Government was overthrown by Fidel Castro's revolution in 1959. The USA did not like that man; there were documented attempts to get him murdered by the CIA, and Cuba had to endure years of economic hardship through embargoes. Their revolution was called socialism, but because of economic hardship, they called for help from communist Russia, which ended in the infamous Cuban Missile Crisis, nearly leading to war between USA and Russia in 1962.

Somehow Cuba survived, but a lot of help is needed. Many Cubans exiled in the USA would be able and willing to help their families and friends in Cuba but are being cut off through harsh penalties by the USA in case they break the embargoes imposed. Generations of Cuban people have suffered but would be very capable of improving their own lives and others if only given a chance. Their only survival is based mainly on their export of tobacco products, rum and sugar. In later years the tourist trade has become a significant contributor to the GDP of Cuba. Another income generator seems to be the exportation of medical expertise in the form of Cuban-trained doctors and nurses who are being sent to foreign countries to earn cash for themselves and the Cuban Government. Since they all have been trained by the Cuban Government free of charge, they only get a small percentage of the salary earned overseas; the rest is paid into the government coffers to repay their education.

I believe Cuba will not need help once normal economic activities are possible. Lift the embargo, and let the families and friends on both sides of the dividing water help each other improve the lives of the ordinary people in Cuba.

The only contribution I can make is to continue my support for the Cuban tobacco farmers by smoking their beautiful cigars. Unfortunately, I cannot extend this help to the very sweet Mojito ingredients of rum and sugar to preserve the delicate balance of my health and enjoyment.

Viva la Cuba

Political motivation was never on my mind. Growing up in a city divided into the Communist East and the Capitalistic West we were always bombarded with propaganda from both sides.

Youthful Folly

The mix of facts and fiction made it impossible to form an educated opinion and being only seventeen years old there were plenty of more pressing distractions: Dancing school to learn how to become a gentleman, going to commercial school to learn the theory of how to run a business and being involved in the Boy Scout movement to teach some cubs how to survive in the wilderness.

But there was one thing which got our attention. Once a week several friends and I had to take the train to go to our school. Although we travelled in the West part of town, the train was under the administration of the Communist East. A strange arrangement made during the time the Allies divided the city to keep control of the population. To compensate, the underground trains were totally run by the Western administration.

Rattling along in the run-down carriage, we had to pass an area which used to be a maintenance yard for the trains with several rails and switches not being needed any more. For a reason I still do not understand the rail department kept some personnel in the old building which housed the operation centre for the switching yard. They had absolutely nothing to do as the few trains per day just trundled past in a straight line.

One day we noticed a flag which had been hoisted on a water tank tower next to the old building. It was big and was clearly identified as a banner of the FDJ *(Freie Deutsche Jugend)* or Free German Youth movement organised by the Communist Party of East Germany. A lively discussion took place amongst us. None of us had political ambitions, but we certainly did not agree that a Communist flag should be so flagrantly displayed in West Berlin. The argument that it was actually in the Communist controlled rail yard did not stick with us. The local newspapers commented on this affront and there was a strong opinion that this was something the authorities should take up with the Communist administration. There was no chance for that; the FDJ flag kept on fluttering in the wind, to the annoyance of most travellers passing by.

It was a warm summer night. My mother was away visiting family, my brothers were working already in West Germany and I built up this feeling that something had to be done to show that not everything dished out by the Communists would be tolerated.

A long bus journey took me to the rail yard that night. I knew the water tower was near the old building and that would be a challenge, as the lights inside told me it was manned for whatever reason. The fence around the rail yard did not pose any problem, the few wires left were easily pushed aside, and I entered the yard, moving over many old railway lines towards the tower. That brought up another question. How to negotiate so many railway lines if I needed to run away when it was so dark one could hardly see a hand in front of its own face.

I finally skirted the old building and faced the tower. It had been damaged during the war and sharp metal bits sticking out had to be negotiated. Close by, the flag looked even bigger, and it became obvious that I could not untie the flag pole from the metal tower. My entire plan and the long journey were in jeopardy. At least I had to have a try to do something. As a boy scout we had these old leather short pants as a uniform and I was wearing those. These pants had a small sleeve on the bottom and I had safely hidden a razor blade inside the sleeve just in case it would be needed.

Tonight was the night. I checked for any movements in the old building, as the light illuminated the tower on one side. There was nothing I could do about it but hope that anybody looking out of the building would be blinded by their own light and would miss any action on the tower.

Slowly I climbed up the metal structure, avoiding the sharp pieces of metal sticking out. Once I reached the bottom of the flag, attached to a very heavy and securely attached flag pole, I made sure I had a firm grip on the tower with one hand. My other hand went for the razor blade in the pant sleeve and I tried to reach up to the flag. Too short, either my arm or my legs; I could not touch the flag. Putting away the blade for safety I somehow overcame my sweaty fear and heaved myself up another cross section of the tower construction. A quick look at the lights in the building and I felt assured that so far nobody had noticed my actions.

The razor blade started cutting only the lower part of the flag but it allowed me to rip most of the flag away from the pole so that it was hanging only on the last threads at the top. Further action could have been foolish as I did not know if the people in the building might do some nightly rounds of inspection.

I cut a small piece off the flag which I stuffed into my pocket. The climb down was in haste but I always kept a good look around in case somebody would apprehend me. Safely on the ground I forced myself not to run, as that could have easily resulted in a broken leg when negotiating the railway lines in the dark. Slipping through the fence line I finally inhaled a good load of air without having to worry about being heard.

The ride back on the bus is a bit of a blur for me. I know I must have been grinning a lot but the strange looks of other passengers must have had something to do with the fact that I was absolutely filthy. The climb up the tower, hugging the rusty iron mixed with my sweat must have given me a frightful look, although being almost clad like a boy scout I got away with it.

Finally at home, I needed a good shower followed by a relaxing sleep. The small piece of the flag was pegged to the a little board next to my bed, the razor blade was back in the pants sleeve, all secure.

The following week my friends and I passed the rail yard again, as every week. I had told nobody about my little excursion as there was always the thought of communist spies wandering around in West Berlin, too many stories had been circulating and I would not gloat over what I had done only to end up being kidnapped and punished by the Communists.

One fellow actually noticed that the infamous flag was in tatters and wondered if there had been a storm during the last few days. No comment from me as I blended inconspicuously with the group of speculators.

The Sydney Opera House and a German ship called 'Helgoland' was the trigger for my interest in Vietnam.

Yes, that sounds somewhat odd, but please hear me out.

I have to go back to my early school days in Berlin. Every morning a friend and I toddled off on a long walk to attend classes in the Primary School. This fellow, Wolfgang, annoyed me frequently by talking too much and, whilst doing that, pushing closer and closer until I felt crammed and moved to his other side. That ended up one day in a small fistfight, but no harm was done. We actually became good friends and spent many hours after school playing around.

Wolfgang's father was hardly present, being a busy architect and professor of acoustics. I did not know what that was.

Many years later, I ended up in Sydney after a long journey with another friend, taking us overland through the Middle East until we were stopped by the unfriendly activities between Pakistan and India. That was in late autumn 1965. Pure luck and a little patience gave us the chance to catch a cargo ship offering twelve berths to passengers. Our final destination was Sydney, where we arrived in January 1966.

A few months passed by before a suitable position was secured in a small branch office of the company in which I had undergone my training back in Germany some years before.

The Sydney Opera House featured daily in the news. Problems between the famous architect Jørn Utzon and the New South Wales' Government, financial problems which resulted in a weekly Lottery to use the proceeds to continue building the project and issues of construction and acoustics. At that stage, overseas consultants were called in, including Lothar Cremer and Professor Werner Gabler. They had built up a reputation in Europe for fixing similar issues in various concert halls. Professor Gabler's son, Wolfgang, gave me some details, and I managed to arrange a meeting with the professor in Sydney. Nothing of the discussion sticks in my mind except for one thing: The older sister of my friend Wolfgang had become a doctor. She had volunteered to serve on a German hospital ship tied up in the port of Saigon in Vietnam. Apparently, the sister contracted a tropical disease and was shipped home.

That whole story, short of details at it was, got my attention. The news on Vietnam and the continuing war just passed over my head; I had no radio or TV and was more interested in earning more cash to pay the rent. But what were the Germans up to in a war, which in my mind, was an American and Australian problem. Since Mr Google did not exist in those days, the questions faded away as no answer was available. Even though Vietnam became more focused in my observations of what was going on in the world.

It was 1968, only a couple of years later, when I had my next reminder that Vietnam was in a state of war.

My engagement in the company gave me more opportunities to travel, even if it was only for business purposes. After a long meeting in Head Office Frankfurt, I boarded a flight to Hong Kong. Pan American Airlines operated two round the world flights daily, one in each direction, west and east. Operated with Boeing 707 planes, the range was not exactly stunning by our present measures. The journey required going to many places on the way to drop off and pick up passengers. The languages, clothing, smells and food offered changed almost at every stop to cater to different nationalities. After Istanbul, Beirut, and Bombay, I had given up noticing anything; tired and uncomfortable with the long flight and many stops, I just wanted to get off the plane in Hong Kong and have a shower and some decent food.

The pilot announced we would soon leave our cruising height, and it was a relief that the torture would be over soon. Descending towards the airport and looking out the window, I noticed a different countryside from what I expected. Green fields looked like rice paddies, with plenty of aircraft in the air, and finally, it became clear. This was not Hong Kong. Soon it became clear that we had landed at Saigon Airport, in the middle of the war zone. Some people got off, but all other passengers had to stay on board. Two burly American Military Police with machine guns were posted on the door. The small distance to what was a terminal building was guarded by a couple of Jeeps mounted with guns which looked capable of delivering plenty of firepower. The heat and humidity crept into the plane, external air conditioners were unavailable, and the on-board system could not cope since the engines were switched off. Three hours can be a very long time on the tarmac, providing a large target for anybody who cared to take a shot at us.

The long waiting time allowed the opportunity to look around outside, at least from various windows. Not a pleasant view of a tropical paradise. On every corner of the taxiways, anti-aircraft guns were emplaced. Solid concrete bunkers had been built all over the airfield to shelter the many aircraft based there. Strings of large helicopters were hovering around, forming groups before dashing off in one or the other direction. Bombers took off in pairs, circling overhead until they had enough numbers to go for whatever they wanted to bomb. Immediately after that, several jet fighters took off to follow the bombers, providing cover if an unfriendly fighter pilot had the idea of strafing the bombers. To make things more worrisome, one could see many bombed or burned out metal structures strewn over the field, which resembled vehicles, helicopters and even the odd larger aircraft. We were told this was due to the efforts of the Vietcong, who sent mortar bombs over the fence every so often.

I really didn't fancy spending too much time on the ground in those conditions. Luckily even three hours of anxiety will pass, eventually. The wheels up after take-off could not have become sooner.

The final approach to Kai Tak Airport in Hong Kong provided the last rush of adrenalin. We turned sharply before a huge rock painted in red and white for better visibility. In that final turn, one could see the washing hanging out on top of the buildings, just down from the wing tips, before the plane straightened up and almost crash-landed on the runway to ensure a stop was achieved before the wet harbour was reached. Those landings in Hong Kong were never dull.

One thing I promised myself when finally enjoying the long shower in a hotel; I needed to read up about Vietnam, get some picture of what the country and people were all about, and try to understand the stupidity which was going on right then in a place I unknowingly had to visit in transit.

The completion of the Sydney Opera House took another five years, until October 1973, but that was the least important fact on my mind. Work was exciting and demanding; getting married in 1969 distracted me even more from taking notice of political events, and the subsequent move to Perth threw me back into a more provincial surrounding, which affected the way people looked at the world stage from the isolation of WA.

Australia had been involved in the Vietnam War for some years, being a close ally of America. In 1969/70, the public opposed sending soldiers into a war they thought was not winnable. Demonstrations against the war were increasingly reported in the news, and even I took more notice of what was happening in Vietnam.

My unexpected landing in Saigon a couple of years earlier became more significant. The devastation I noticed on the ground at Saigon airport apparently directly resulted from the 'Tet' offensive by the Viet Cong in early 1968. Tet is the equivalent of the Chinese New Year, which usually is associated with family reunions, holidays and the celebration of a New Year's arrival. That year the Viet Cong surprised the Allied Forces by launching this offensive during that holiday period with no prior sign or warning. Although they were finally beaten back, their action left a clear message to all warring parties involved; the continuation of this war would cost more casualties and vast amounts of money, and politicians began to worry about their jobs. The voters were totally unhappy, and plans emerged to implement a withdrawal from the action by giving the local South Vietnamese Army more responsibility in fighting their war.

Having grown up in Berlin during and immediately after WWII, I understood the background of what was happening in Vietnam. Western countries versus Communist Countries.

North Vietnam was being influenced and supported by China and Russia. South Vietnam got assistance from America with the support of allied nations to stem the expansion of the communist influence. Initially, there were no open hostilities between the North and South Vietnam, but I believe the Viet Cong in the South began an insurgency to prepare for the overthrow of the South Vietnamese government, which North Vietnam covertly supported until direct confrontation took place.

OK, finally, my head was more attuned to the news covering Vietnam, but there was still the mystery of why and how the Germans got involved in the war. It took quite a long time to get to know the background of all that.

America pushed their western allies to support their effort in fighting this war in Vietnam. Germany did not want to take part in any military action but promised to help with humanitarian aid.

A pleasure boat called the 'Helgoland' was ferrying weekend holidaymakers to the island of Helgoland.

Germany decided to convert this vessel into a hospital ship and sent it to Vietnam in 1966.

The entire project was under the flag of the Red Cross and the Geneva Convention. Designated as totally neutral, the operation was conducted within strict rules to only treat patients who were not military personnel. Supplies came in from Germany under a special agreement with the South Vietnamese government with a minimum of scrutiny, paying no taxes or duties.

The ship was staffed with ten doctors and 30 nurses and included three operating rooms and a fully-functioning laboratory. Some 150 hospital beds were available to treat patients. Over the entire period of this humanitarian engagement, some 10,000 operations took place; over 200,000 out-patients were treated, and over 230,000 laboratory tests were conducted. The mission ended in 1971 when a land-based hospital was established to more efficiently cater to people in need. (All this information is courtesy of Wikipedia.)

This was the ship Professor Gabler referred to in Sydney when telling me the story of his daughter, who contracted a tropical disease whilst carrying out her duties and was evacuated back to Germany.

The impact of the work done on board soon prompted the local population to call the 'Helgoland' the 'White Ship of Hope'.

My curiosity about why the German government got involved in Vietnam was finally satisfied. A sad end of this story was the news that all the German staff at the land-based hospital were captured during the final push of the Viet Cong into South Vietnam and later murdered. These horrors only came to light many years later, when many books on the war were published. One of the most gruesome stories published was the history of the 'Tunnel Rats or Tunnel Ferret'; they described the incredible feats of soldiers trying to eliminate the enemy forces inside the extensive tunnel system dug by the Viet Cong. The purpose of the tunnels was to deliver supplies and conduct armed raids right from under the American base outside Saigon (Cu Chi Tunnels). All these details only emerged many years later and were not known by me when I just simply concentrated on the job on hand, making a living.

In 1976, I took on a new position, as country manager in Taiwan. By that time, the first Vietnamese refugees had arrived in various countries. The war in Vietnam had come to a close after total victory by the North Vietnamese army over the South Vietnam forces. The government had collapsed, and even the dramatic last-minute evacuation efforts by the allied forces could not solve the problem of those afraid of being prosecuted by the new regime. Many were left behind and were rightly worried about their lives. Those who had some money could charter fishing vessels to flee their country, ending up in many Asian countries if they survived that perilous journey. Many died when their boat sank, others were taken by pirates and robbed of their possessions, and many were slaughtered afterwards. News of these atrocities spurred a considerable effort to settle those refugees wherever possible.

All this had little impact on our daily routine in Taiwan until one day, I inspected our small warehouse near the office. We had many export shipments of cartons full of textiles and shoes manufactured in Taiwan. In what seemed to be a comfortable surrounding, I found a Vietnamese gentleman and his wife who had taken shelter in our warehouse. He was helping our staff with some minor tasks and stayed in the warehouse for lack of alternative accommodation. I found out that he was a member of a large Vietnamese family. They were sent off on boats by the father, with some cash or gold bars, to survive whenever they could find a safe harbour. I could not find a proper solution at the time but decided to ignore the issues involved by just allowing this man and his wife to stay in our warehouse for the time being, until he got officially accepted as a refugee. Apparently, his other siblings and mother were waiting to be processed as refugees in a camp in Malaysia. I found out recently that the father also got out of Vietnam. He was able to get his whole family settled in America.

Through contacts in Taiwan, I heard that the couple, sheltered in our warehouse, are now happy grandparents and are doing well in the USA.

On one of my trips to Hong Kong, I had to go to the German Consulate to apply for a new passport. The office was hectic, to say the least; the official informed me it could take weeks before my application could be processed because of a massive influx of refugees from Vietnam trying to get approval to go to Germany. As there was no official representation of Germany in Taiwan, I persuaded the official to put me in first as the entire trip to Hong Kong was purely to get a new passport. I could not wait around for so long. It worked, but a lot of grumbling by the overworked official could be heard.

My time in Taiwan ended because of some changes in international politics, which resulted in the closure of the American school in Taipei. As a result, my children needed a place to be educated. Therefore, I had to accept a move to Singapore, where there were several choices of educational institutes suitable for their age and long-term aim.

Singapore was home for four years, and then it was back to Perth to settle the children into the local education system.

Only two years later, I ended up in Hong Kong to lead the office of another German forwarder to take over responsibilities in South East Asia, including China. Although I had travelled a lot on business due to my functions in Singapore, I had never visited Vietnam, which was still not able or willing to open up for business after the war ended in 1975.

I had no chance to get a more personal impression of the people and the country during all that time. Then, years later, I received an invitation from a close friend in Hong Kong, Captain Tommy Lam, to join a group of 50 Taiwanese and four Hong Kong business people to visit Vietnam; I happily accepted.

The Government in Vietnam had to get their country back on its feet. A new policy was announced to open up for business by introducing a socialist-orientated market economy *(Doi Moi)*. It hoped to get overseas investors to help start some 200 projects, all considered essential and viable for the immediate future. Our group of Chinese entrepreneurs was put together by a Vietnamese gentleman in America. He apparently fled Saigon just before the takeover by the North Vietnamese Army in 1975.

It felt strange to be the only non-Chinese participant in the group, but because of my previous time in Taiwan, I was quite at home dealing with most of the different characters.

The task of getting all the documents together to apply for the visa indicated what to expect, and arriving at Hanoi Airport, more official papers had to be prepared. In addition, a detailed list of cash on hand and valuables such as cameras, watches, and other expensive items were required. Strangely enough, there was no inspection of those items listed, but the reason for that became apparent later. Vietnam was not worried about getting cash or other valuables into the country, but on leaving, they wanted to make sure that you did not take out more than what you declared on arrival. We thought it was all very different, but it made sense as many citizens still tried to get funds out of Vietnam to create a new life overseas.

The immigration inspection was almost laughable and reminded me of the past years of crossing the East German borders anywhere. Inside a large hall posing as the airport terminal, wooden boxes housed the immigration officers, who inspected all documents at length. A wooden pole barred passage until the official was satisfied that all was in order. Before retracting the wooden pole manually into his hut, he would first look up to scrutinise a large mirror hanging on the outside, in which he could see if somebody was sneaking into the country by hiding below his field of vision. That was exactly what I experienced years ago in East Germany; the training of those border guards in Vietnam had obviously been influenced by their comrades from East Germany.

Finally, we had accomplished all the official parts of entering the country. We now had to search for our luggage. The airport terminal in Hanoi had no air-conditioning. There was no infrastructure to handle the baggage; everybody had to scramble around to find his own piece after the luggage was just dumped on the floor after offloading from the aircraft. Another physical effort was required to drag the bags to the transport waiting outside. Something looked very familiar about those buses. The colour had initially been yellow but changed to brown with a thick layer of reddish-brown dust, which was everywhere, including the inside and on the seats. These vehicles at one time served as school buses for the Americans stationed in

South Vietnam and had now become the official transport for our VIP delegation visiting Hanoi in the North.

Just as well, we had prepared ourselves a little by not dressing up in our Sunday best. Our clothing was sure to be filthy within minutes of boarding the bus; our one-hour trip to our hotel increased the level of dust inside as we took several unsurfaced back roads to get to our destination. The reason was clearly the fact that there was only one bridge spanning the Red River in Hanoi, and we had to take a long detour to reach our hotel. The Long Bien Bridge had also been damaged during the war, including most roads leading towards Hanoi. Only one lane was open, and over the distance of 1.6 km, we all prayed that we would not meet any ongoing traffic. It would have been an interesting exercise trying to unravel any resulting traffic jam. Our hotel, called Thang Loi, was built and gifted from the communist comrades in Cuba to the Government of Vietnam; it became the official hotel for arriving VIPs.

The large reception area was filled with our group and luggage, and it took quite an effort to get our rooms sorted out. They were small rooms with a private shower and toilet and even had a simple TV in the corner for your entertainment. The design of the place was quite interesting as all the rooms were facing the big lake, but to access them required a long hike along a corridor which actually was a pier built over the water's edge. The actual entertainment was not the program on the TV but the fact that the cabling was faulty; walking barefoot on the stone floor after a shower gave you a worrying tingly feeling which stopped only when you pulled the electric plug out of the wall socket. You learn quickly in situations like that.

The view from the room was idyllic. The lake was quite large and provided many fishers with the opportunity to catch fish any time of the day. Watching several small rowing boats crossing the lake was an interesting sight: one man sitting in the boat, two legs and feet busy rowing the boat, so he had two hands free to handle the fishing rod to cast away. It looked almost weird how they contorted themselves, but it seemed to be efficient enough to handle the rowing and the fishing simultaneously. I called them Spidermen.

The laundry was happily attended to by housekeeping staff since it provided an extra income for them.

You could see them hunching below the rooms on the lake water's edge, washing your clothes by hand and subsequently stringing those items on a rope between the jetty pillars to dry out. But it was very cheap service.

The buses picked us up the next morning for our first official appointment. Dressed in business suits and ties, we were worried that we might look like water buffaloes who just had rolled in wet and red mud after the next ride. But there was no big issue. We must have done a thorough job when sitting in those dust traps the day before; they were almost clean, and we did not have to be embarrassed when getting out at our first stop. Not that our host would have cared much, I wager. He had passed away quite some time ago but was embalmed and displayed in a large white mausoleum in the centre of Hanoi. Ho Chi Minh had been the beloved leader of the Vietnamese people for many years, a teacher by profession but a passionate political leader for most of his later years to achieve freedom from foreign dominance and occupation in Vietnam. It was the correct thing to do, paying our respects before getting involved in high-level business meetings. The mausoleum entrance was guarded by stony-faced soldiers in dress uniform, no cameras were allowed, and talking was discouraged on entering the vast hall from one side. We all filed past the body, looking at the glass coffin from 270 degrees. It was eerie to consider that this servant of his country was being used after his death as a political showcase to keep the masses in awe of what the communist party had achieved under his leadership. It was also irksome to think that the corpse had to be sent to Russia for repeated embalming processes to keep the spectacle going for a long time. That was not a good start to the day, and we were happy the sun was shining outside when leaving the gloomy and darkish mausoleum.

Our next stop was the Ministry of Commerce. Red carpets in front greeted our delegation. We were received by a high-ranking vice minister and ushered into the conference hall. The vice minister and all his aids spoke perfect Chinese, and they all could converse easily. I was left out to a degree but was allocated a particular interpreter who tried hard to explain the proceedings to me in English. The gist of it all was the usual greetings and welcoming us as new friends of Vietnam in the hope the business people would invest in one of the 200 projects which were presented to us. The range of investment opportunities was vast. Power projects, railway projects, textile factories, shoe factories, cement factories, anything which a country needed to get out of its economic hole after the terrible war, which had obliterated the livelihood of most of the population. Help was offered to cut down the red tape to get these projects underway. But it did not take long to understand that this was not a simple task. Basically, anyone would have to bring their own money, take the total risk, but still be under the control and supervision of the authorities. There was very little skilled labour available; every raw material would have to be imported and accounted for on export. Immense problems would arise when writing off wastages and losses due to production problems. The bureaucratic powers in charge were incapable of understanding or managing such a tremendous task. Upstream production of textiles or shoes could not start until the basics were available, like yarns, leather and accessories, none of which was available locally. For me, as a forwarder, it painted a rosy picture. I imagined the enormous volume of shipments to be transported into the country and subsequently looked at the exports of those commodities.

The following lunch at a simple local seafood restaurant provided sustenance essential to the body and plenty of time for detailed discussions within the group. Some members of the group were impressed and contemplated how they would get the first steps organised; others were quite pessimistic about the problems facing them. But all the manufacturers from Taiwan had a common problem. Their products were becoming too expensive because of rising labour costs in their home country, so they needed to look at new and cheaper places to start factories and continue prospering in the ever-changing international market.

There was nothing available in terms of entertainment for the visitors. But the Chinese are enterprising men, and a small group found out that they could get away from their official accommodation to do some exploring on their own in town. Little coffee shops in small side streets provided a cosy atmosphere, sitting in the street on tiny little chairs manufactured from reeds. What else went on there? I could not tell because I was not included in those excursions, which obviously were not condoned by our hosts. The Chinese could blend in like locals, but I would have stuck out like a sore thumb since I could not hide my non-Asian face.

Saturday night was an exception. The hotel put on a weekly dance with a live band. One member of that band was a German from the East German Embassy, which still existed in 1988, before the collapse of East Germany. The attraction was that local ladies could join the dance without paying an entrance fee, and my Chinese compatriots took full advantage of that.

I believe some ladies managed to earn good money by leading the way to the rooftop, which was littered with chairs and benches, and again I could only guess what went on. Considering all, it was a great night with dances and plenty of local beer to drench the thirst after a long, humid day.

Another official excursion was the visit to the War Museum in Hanoi. Obviously, it was meant to impress everybody on how Vietnam struggled to defend itself against its enemies and achieve the eventual victory. One has to understand the history of Vietnam to see why all this is important. In fact, Vietnam has been under foreign suppression for several hundred years. Chinese, Mongols, and Thais in the earlier years, followed by French colonisation. Without going into many details, it was clear to see that the struggle of Vietnam has always been to become independent from foreign occupation. They are proud of finally having achieved that after the second Vietnam War, even at a terrible loss of life and hardship for years to come.

I would highly recommend reading up about Vietnam's history. It gives a totally different perspective of the country and people over several hundred years.

Several meetings with government companies did not really impress the group; it became clear there was no room for entrepreneurs, as every aspect of the economy was centrally controlled by the powers in charge. But there were signs that a change would be welcomed, even if it took a little more time.

The departure next morning was not a merry occasion. Loud knocks on the doors at 4 am woke us, and we all assembled in the entrance hall to be shuffled to our buses. The departure was set for 6 am. The one hour drive to the airport was a race on the dykes, following the Red River and negotiating bad roads full of potholes. Again we crossed the famous old bridge to get over the river and finally arrived at the airport. Being a domestic flight, there were few formalities, and we just scrambled across the tarmac to board an old Russian plane. No seats were allocated, and while a lot of the group were still trying to find an empty seat, the aircraft moved off. Seatbelts were not available, and thick mist filled the plane when the two ancient engines started up. Experts assured us it was only the condensation which formed after the aircraft had stood on the tarmac overnight in the humid air of Hanoi. The first few minutes of the flight were an agonising experience. At very low speed, the plane only gained altitude after some minutes, when every passenger finally breathed again. Just as well, there are no hills around Hanoi Airport; I would not be here to tell the story as we would not have been able to clear any obstacle. A second plane followed us immediately to complete the regularly scheduled cattle run to Ho Chi Minh City of the day.

Ho Chi Minh City, previously called Saigon, was a total contrast to Hanoi.

Descending toward the airport, one could already smell the humid air awaiting us on the tarmac. It was a strange feeling landing at the same airport I involuntarily visited 20 years ago. Nothing much had changed as far as I could make out. The damaged aircraft shelters next to the runway were still there. The arrival hall looked from the outside as if nothing had been added since I saw it the last time, except the war wrecks of vehicles, aircraft and helicopters had been cleared off the field. Some holes showed where the anti-aircraft guns had been embedded. As our travel had been domestic, the passengers were not subjected to any obvious scrutiny, and we could get our luggage from an ancient conveyor belt to drag outside. The provided buses matched those we had been using in Hanoi but did not display the same amount of red dust, as the roads had not been bombed or blown up during the long period of the war as they had in North Vietnam. The contrast was also visible in other areas. Hanoi was backwards, with few shops and little traffic on the roads. But the communist system had the advantage that they were organised, kept their appointments, and it was easy to get around. Ho Chi Minh City (HCMC) was a typically bustling, hot South-East Asian town with some cars and thousands of little motorcycles crowding the streets. The noise level was a constant irritant, and the whole scene appeared messy and dirty.

Saigon was known to have several famous hotels. Surely now, in HCMC, the same hotels should be available to accommodate us with a far better comfort than the simple Thang Loi Hotel in Hanoi. Unfortunately, this was not the case. For reasons that only sank in later, we all had to be quartered in large houses that had previously belonged to the American personnel stationed in Saigon.

It was quite a logistical nightmare to ferry 54 group members to some 15 different locations using the same buses which picked us up at the airport. My friend Tommy Lam and I were billeted in a large room, with two more rooms occupied by other travellers. The owner and host of this establishment was a retired high-ranking military officer from either the North Vietnam Army or the Viet Cong; we never found out which. That appeared to be the pattern; all American houses were given to loyal supporters of the new government. Since cash was king, they were allowed to rent rooms to visiting VIPs to earn extra money.

After a few days, we realised that the few hotels in the city were still operating in some ways, but we had to stay in the houses to support the veterans.

It always takes me at least one night to get used to new surroundings when I lay my head down. This time it took even longer. I am not used to sharing a room with a stranger, even though it was my good friend Tommy. It was pretty scary when I slowly came to in the first morning light to hear loud puffing and huffing. In my hazed mind, I was convinced that we were staying at a railway station and a steam train was approaching in proximity. Just as well, one can wake up from those nightmares. It turned out that Tommy was a keen follower of *Tai Chi*, the ancient Chinese art of exercising the body and mind. That involves heavy breathing to clear the lungs and mind of impurities, hence the heavy puffing. Tommy was not a smoker but keen to have a glass of beer or wine, which may have contributed to the noisy efforts the next morning.

An official program in HCMC followed the same routine as we experienced in Hanoi. A reception was held at the City Hall, which was now the seat of the Chairman of the People's Committee of Ho Chi Minh City. The red carpet may not have been as clean as the one in Hanoi, but the speeches and the warm welcome to invest in the same 200 projects offered in Hanoi did not change at all. Again the language spoken was Chinese (Mandarin). My interpreter was quite at ease translating to English, which he mastered very well, although with a slight American accent. He must have been working with the Americans stationed in Saigon before the fall of the South Vietnam Government.

In situations like that, you only catch up with the most interesting points later. Chinese language and writing were still forbidden in Vietnam. No Chinese restaurant could show a menu written in Chinese. However, here we were, officially briefed on the brand new world of Vietnam, all in the

Chinese language. Remarkable. What was even more curious was the fact that we met in the official premises of the previous Mayor of the City of Saigon. Our Vietnamese leader of the group occupied that position just before he finally managed to flee to the USA before the fall of Saigon. Now we were sitting in his old office facilities talking to the new leader with the official title of Chairman, performing the same function. It appeared to me that they were good friends, and therefore it was no surprise to see both gentlemen joining us for a Chinese dinner that night. Once again, the changes in society became obvious. Menus are written in Chinese, and a rock band, clad in artificial leather outfits making a lot of western-style noises; that certainly was a totally new trend in a country that had condemned any cultural trends originating in America.

The local arrangements included visiting the Cu Chi tunnels outside HCMC. During the war against North Vietnam, the Americans had a large base close to the city from where they coordinated their actions against the North and the insurgency of the Viet Cong. The irony became clear when the existence of the tunnels became known. The Viet Cong had dug a vast system underneath the American base, small tunnels which could only be conversed by small and almost crawling men. Those tunnels opened up into sleeping quarters well below the ground. They included simple hospitals, command centres and canteens to provide food for the fighters living in those conditions. There was only one problem: cooking. The smell of preparing food had to be ventilated without being detected by the American guards controlling the camp above. The tunnel system was actually quite a stroke of genius. Where to hide best but right underneath the enemy? They could emerge through tiny hatches directly into the camp, cause havoc, and disappear back into the tunnels without leaving a trace. Later Australian and American Special Forces were formed to take the fight to the Vietnam inside their tunnels. Some gruesome stories about the incredible conditions of those underground skirmishes have been written in many books. If the reader is interested, I would highly recommend reading the history of the so-called Tunnel Rats. But don't switch off the lights after reading the book; you may not sleep too well.

Vietnam was negatively affected by an event which took place in Berlin, Germany, in November 1989. The infamous Berlin Wall was finally demolished, signalling the first important step in the reunification of East and West Germany.

For many years Germany allowed Vietnamese citizens to live and work in East Germany. Officially over 200,000 Vietnamese spent two to three years in Germany, receiving an education and learning German. Many took on apprenticeships in industries such as the manufacturers of motorcars, trucks and simple farm machinery. Some estimates also quote up to 500,000 Vietnamese nationals who lived and worked in Germany at one stage or the other. With the demise of East Germany as a state, large-scale repatriation of Vietnamese had to take place as their legal status in Germany had changed overnight; many avoided their return by trying to seek asylum in reunited Germany. The integration of East and West Germany presented many problems, not the least of which were of a financial nature. To my knowledge, there was not much consideration for the Vietnamese in Germany and many stayed on illegally to avoid the return to their home country.

For Vietnam, it provided new commercial problems as there were hardly any jobs available which could be offered to the returnees. The government policy of opening up the economy to foreign investment was still new. It did not show the desired effect as quickly as had been hoped. Investors were still struggling with the immense task of starting new ventures as the expectations of the government was not in a realistic time frame considering there was a lack of everything; trained workers, regulations and laws, raw materials and infrastructure. The timing of the collapse of East Germany came just at the wrong moment for Vietnam; the struggle for survival was made even more difficult because aid received from East Germany naturally stopped.

In late 1990, the German Hong Kong Business Association decided to explore new opportunities in Vietnam. A team of business experts was assembled to visit Vietnam and hold Seminars for members of the Vietnamese local business chapters in Hanoi and HCMC. The aim was to bring the local business community up to date on international trade and make contacts, which, hopefully, would result in a future profitable business relationship.

My earlier visit to Vietnam and my particular expertise in the transport field earned me an invitation to join this educational trip; mind you, every participant still had to pay for their own expenses. By now, a routine had been established in which official visits were organised by the Vietnam authorities. Fly into Hanoi, stay in the Thang Loi Hotel as we had before, and make the rounds to visit various government departments and state companies. Then fly to HCMC for some more of the same. No more red carpet; it must have worn out by that time as many international delegations had visited in the past eighteen months; everybody was keen to learn how to increase their profits by investing in Vietnam, only to realise that this would require a lot of patience, money and strong nerves.

The local equivalent of a Chamber of Commerce in Hanoi presented us to their members. We tried to give them some insight into what they would have to do, learn and execute if they wanted to do international business. It could take the form of importing raw materials and manufacturing items such as shoes, textiles and clothing, which were very labour intensive and attractive to Vietnam to get the employment level up. My contribution involved the mechanics of import and export shipping, documentation and advice on what customs regulations they would be required to adhere to. Communication was exhausting as English was not exactly well spoken amongst the North Vietnamese community. Some issues must have been very hard for them to understand since the local business people had never had an opportunity to participate in international trade before now.

We had a few interesting encounters as a group.

The German ambassador in Hanoi invited us for cocktails at his residence. It was reassuring to see he was a down to earth and practical person with whom we could openly discuss the issues we were facing. He initially pointed out the advantages German investors might have considering the large pool of German-trained mechanics who had a reasonable ability to speak German.

Unfortunately, the timing again was not right. There was no way a new automobile industry could be created for many years. Enormous investments were needed, and the local market could not support sufficient sales for as long as the median income was close to the poverty line. The positive fact was that all those mechanics had experience with the old East German trucks and cars, of which plenty were running around in Vietnam. When

I said running, I was not being entirely accurate. Those vehicles were old, of poor quality and tended to break down more often than they actually ran. But there was no alternative, and plenty of mechanical expertise was required to keep the wheels in motion (pun intended). Here was the niche where the returned workers became useful in many places.

Another visit was organised by the OAV. Translated, that meant the East Asiatic Association, which was based in Hamburg. Members comprised traditional trading companies with experience and connections in the Far East for a long time. They decided to be present in Vietnam right from the earlier days. They paid for the expenses to maintain a small liaison office in Hanoi to represent the members' interests. It was a surprise for me when I met the manager. He was the young German fellow who played in a band at the Thang Loi Hotel almost two years ago during my visit with the Taiwanese/Hong Kong delegation. Of course, we knew that he previously was a member of staff at the East German Embassy but lost his job when the upheavals in East Germany brought an end to the communist state.

Here he was, all bright and bushy-tailed to represent the capitalistic world in Vietnam. Actually, he was a very pleasant and intelligent young fellow, and I enjoyed his company on several occasions after that meeting in the OAV office.

Our departure for HCMC followed the same path as on my previous trip. A wake-up racket too early in the morning, the somewhat dangerous journey over dykes and that old bridge over the Red River and the two aeroplanes being filled with passengers to take off for the cattle run to HCMC. I was amazed that nothing much had changed in the past couple of years. At least not visible in the country's infrastructure, although there seemed to be more little shops and more small motorcycles in the streets, providing a health hazard when crossing to the other side.

HCMC was different. The accommodation was now provided in hotels, no more private staying in large houses belonging to some retired cadre of the new regime. We stayed in the Continental Hotel, one of the first hotels to be renovated, followed by the Caravel Hotel and the Rex Hotel. All these hotels were within minutes of the City Hall, the seat of the Chairman of the People's Committee of Ho Chi Minh City.

Our contribution to the organised seminars was received well. The Chair of the Chamber of Commerce in HCMC was a very intelligent, helpful lady. I am not mentioning her name in case it might become difficult for her in that political environment (in fact, I have never been able to remember difficult foreign names). We established an excellent base for discussions, got thanked for our attempts to bring some knowledge to the local business community and naturally, we celebrated our new friendship with a light dinner and some heavy beer. The kind lady stayed a lady, abstained from alcohol, and everybody enjoyed themselves.

One unexpected bonus was found on the street in front of the hotel. Some enterprising fellows carried a little wooden box in front of them, holding it up with a string around their neck. Cigarettes, matches and cigars were on offer. Curious as I am, I checked out the cigars. Wow, real Cuban tobacco, handmade and reasonably preserved. How can one resist when the price was only USD 1.00 per stick and these puppies were not exactly small. I indulged and followed it up with a can or two of Heineken beer available for USD 1.00 each.

Some discrete enquiries cleared up a few questions in my head. All Cuban cigars came from Russian ships, which still plied the trade with Vietnam and Cuba. Russian sailors bought the cigars cheaply in Cuba and then sold them to the local entrepreneurs or maybe had a barter trade of some sort going on. The price of only USD 1.00 was explained later. There was a thriving black market for USD going on, and although it was a cheap price to foreigners, those US dollars went a long way for the locals if changed on the black market. I had been approached a few times on the street to sell my USD but remembering my previous experience with the authorities when leaving Saigon airport, I did not fall into that trap. Better being poor than imprisoned.

During one of our visits to local manufacturers, we found one that produced porcelain elephants. There were various shapes and colours and the most popular had its trunk elevated to the sky.

It was called the Greeting Elephant, and it became the group's favourite. Somehow my travel companions must have paid some attention to what I talked about during our seminars. They recognised I was some kind of transporter, and before I knew it, I was given the task of buying and shipping a bunch of porcelain elephants from Vietnam to Hong Kong. Promises of eternal thankfulness and of payments to come were given; nothing much I could hold against that.

We all returned to Hong Kong without incident, happy with what we thought we had achieved and definitely richer with the experience and the new friends we had made.

Back in my office in Hong Kong, I duly organised to buy and ship elephants. On arrival in Hong Kong, I stored them in our warehouse for distribution to my grateful travel companions. Well, two of them actually remembered their order during our somewhat inebriated evening in HCMC. I ended up as the proud owner of many elephants, which looked very nice but cluttered up my warehouse. Just as well, Christmas was coming. Traditionally one gave some sort of present in the form of wine or whisky to good customers; this time, they all ended up with a couple of elephants instead. Nobody complained, so it must have been acceptable to my business contacts.

Another lesson learned.

It was a lot of fun travelling around Vietnam, but my conscience told me I needed to get some business out of it because my company footed all the expenses.

I achieved the first step by getting a business deal with a semi-government agency, willing to listen to what I had to say with a view to jointly developing some business. That agency was involved in shipping. They could see some advantages in acting as our agents for general freight movements. After that, appointments were made in Hanoi and HCMC with other state organisations involved in manufacturing basic industrial goods. My intention was to investigate if they could become potential importers of materials and eventually export their products. It all looked very promising.

As flights into Vietnam were limited, a direct connection was not workable. The stopover in Bangkok always required an extra day. Subject to the weather, one could expect traffic jams to and from the airport because sometimes half the highway to the city was under water after heavy rainfalls. Water buffaloes frolicked around the deep ditches filled with muddy water from the flooded roads in some areas.

Arriving in Hanoi was almost like stepping back 50 years after the hustle and bustle of the well-developed metropolis of Bangkok. My lodging in the Thang Loi Hotel was the same as on my previous visits; nothing much had improved. It was a welcome sign to find that taxis had started to operate; but they could only be booked at the various hotels being developed around town.

My first appointment was with some officials of the state electricity company. During our first visit with the Taiwanese delegation, one project mentioned on the long list of possible investments was a power plant which they wished to build. All very good but no money was available for that. What could be done? I must have had a brain flash because I remembered that our company's owners were one of the big utilities in Germany. They also built power plants everywhere, and the latest one was to be built in the old area of East Germany. If that plant could be fired by anthracite coal delivered from Vietnam, there could be the possibility of a barter trade whereby our company would pay for the construction of the power plant in Vietnam against deliveries of high-quality anthracite coal for their yet to be built plant in Germany. I promised to investigate and left in a hurry because I was late to meet my contact in the freight agency in Hanoi.

As mentioned, taxis could not be hired on the road curb. I only had a vague idea of where to go, so I decided to trust a local tri-cart driver to take me there to ensure I would not be too late.

Mr Ng was the man in charge of the agency. He was standing outside the little office and scolded me for being late. I blamed the tri-cart driver who got lost, but I was in the bad books, anyway. The ensuing discussion was brief and to the point. Yes, they were interested in working with me, yes, they would help to contact clients and no, there would be no more time for chit-chat as Mr Ng had made six appointments for me on this day, giving me one hour with each company. I got the impression that it was more important to get to the next appointment on time without taking the opportunity to go into more detailed discussions. You can say whatever you like, but I was totally impressed with the precision of the organisation. We always thought that the communist system did not function too well, but here I was, shuffled around like a piece on a chessboard with great meticulousness. My host would politely talk to me, look at his watch and push me out of the door to make sure I made the next appointment. Repeat that six times with the same precision, and you really start believing that these people are great to work with. Unfortunately, all the talks were meaningless. There was no business to be conducted. Yet!

Promises of keeping in touch were made; I was not very hopeful that we could do a lot in Hanoi in the future.

Mr Ng had already instructed his office in HCMC to assist in getting me in touch with various companies interested in doing overseas business. Many appointments were made, but on arrival, the person I was supposed to see was not in, was sick or came late, claiming some important business he had to attend. My local contact at the HCMC office was not really fussed about that. Obviously, he had plenty of experience with that kind of behaviour. The contrast to Hanoi was amazing. Although there seemed to be more active business happening, the way these people were acting was almost destructive and definitely did not encourage anyone to do some honest business with them.

To be fair, it could have been me. But, instead, this stranger is coming from overseas, telling everybody how good he was and what could be done to improve the fortunes of mutual business once started.

I carefully discussed my dilemma with my friendly lady contact at the HCMC Chamber of Commerce. She explained that business ethics in the South were definitely different from the North, but, all had the same problem: no money, no business and still far too many regulations to deal with. Only hard work and time would change that situation, if corruption did not stifle any efforts made in the right direction. Not much I could say, but my thanks were genuine, and I conveyed my intention to be back soon.

I still had to fulfil my promise to the Hanoi electricity company. The utility, our mother company, had a representative based in Singapore and his task was to trade in coal. I was almost an expert on trading in coal as we had to find that commodity under great difficulties during my childhood in Berlin. A coal-fired hearth was all we had; coal was expensive, so we had to find inventive ways to get our hands on it. Some fell off a truck, and some had to be earned by working for somebody. It was almost like a barter trade.

My ideas on how to do business on the ground in Vietnam became more of a reality when I was approached by our sister company to give some help to establish their representative office in HCMC. Technically I was helping my competitors, but since both our companies were owned by the same organisation in Germany, it was a compromise on my behalf to get a foot in the door in Vietnam.

My very helpful lady friend in the Chamber of Commerce in HCMC was receptive to my request for help. I had given detailed information about our corporate structure and the mighty investment power of various corporate member companies. So this was the right push to get approvals from the People's Committee of HCMC.

A German representative, Mr Casper, was placed in the office of a local agent and his task was to look out for business opportunities and co-ordinate any operation which may come up. He had no problem suggesting that I would use his presence in Vietnam to get some marketing done on my own. I could now claim to be represented in Vietnam to persuade future customers to entrust us with setting up a logistic system to handle their future shipments.

My agent in Korea expressed an interest in visiting Vietnam with me to check out what Korean companies were already doing in the country. Some manufacturing of padded jackets had already moved from Bangladesh to Vietnam by some Korean companies. All raw materials had to be imported to Vietnam from Korea as there was no upstream manufacturing of those products in Vietnam yet. The finished products would then be exported worldwide, and this scenario provided great opportunities for our joint companies.

Another German friend of mine in Hong Kong, Helmut Unkel, decided to join us. He was looking for raw materials he wanted to import from Vietnam, mainly carbon black.

I did a bit of planning, and after a short meeting in Hong Kong, we flew to HCMC to meet with Mr Casper to brief him on what we were trying to achieve on this trip. Some appointments were made with local enterprises, which all helped to understand the present state of the fledging economy. Our little group was quite interesting. Two Germans and one Korean travelling in Vietnam, sharing every meal and discussing our impressions and ideas openly. Well, at least we Germans did. My Korean agent was friendly and open, but it was challenging to read his thoughts. Asians think differently from us, and Koreans have been known for being very efficient and pushy in their work environment. Still, in a social situation, they become totally different people.

One evening we decided to follow the concierge's advice in our hotel to visit a local dancing competition. From my past experience in one of the dance halls, I knew the Vietnamese people had a passion for dancing. This event promised to be interesting.

Our car dropped us off at what looked like a round sports arena. Seating was arranged around the centre, there was no roof, and the heat and humidity were accelerated by the large number of spectators filling the stadium. It hadn't really sunk in before, but we were attending a competition by local dance enthusiasts who must have practiced many hours to perfect the *lambada*. The dance was electrifying through its rhythm, and the various movements were definitely sensual and stimulating. The fact that they were allowed to perform this dance in a competition surprised me, as it was only a few years since the opening up to cultural imports of such nature. It was almost comical, but at the same time, sad to see the competitors all dressed up in what they thought would represent an authentic South American outfit. Funny because of the strange combinations and colours, sad because it was apparent that these tattered garments were old and put together from off-cuts and clothing discarded years ago. The competitors made up for everything through their enthusiastic performances. It sometimes resembled acrobatics, which looked almost dangerous but very sexy.

Despite all the fun we had, it was time to leave. The humidity, heat and noise got too much for us, being a somewhat older generation, and we retreated to an air-conditioned bar to cool down with a few Heineken beers.

Our next stop on this trip was Hanoi. Mr Ng, my local agent, had made several appointments for us, which were handled similarly to my previous visit. Efficient, non-productive in terms of actual business, but nevertheless of interest as the main reason for this visit was to gain a better understanding of how the system works (or not) and gain an insight into the daily problems a newcomer to this country would experience when setting up a business.

We were also pleased with the help we got from Mr Casper in HCMC and departed Vietnam with the thought that we had a promising future developing new business with this gentleman's help in the country.

How wrong can one be? And maybe, naïve. The competitiveness and ambitions of some country managers in the sister company put a spanner in the works. My Korean agent was from one of the more prominent companies in direct competition with our sister company in Korea. A formal complaint to Head Office was made, a directive to Mr Casper followed which clearly instructed him not to co-operate with any company outside the group, and I had to ask my agent in Korea for his understanding that he could not count on any help from Mr Casper in the future.

I was embarrassed and fed up. I was put into a difficult situation by our company and had to find solutions, if any were available. Maybe it is helpful to explain more of the background.

For years I ran our office in Hong Kong and developed agencies in all Asian countries to help us provide services to our customers. Let's call our company R with the parent company based in Germany.

Then the parent company bought our competition S in Germany, which had many more branches overseas. It was decided that R would keep doing business as in the past, and the same was said for S, although financially, both companies were merged. In practice, this was not workable as we inevitably came across each other in some business areas as competitors. My attempt to cross the bridge in Vietnam failed, and I had no choice, the knives had to come out, not physically but mentally; I needed to distance my sympathetic feeling for S by making a clean cut and sticking to my network.

Easier said than done. It took a few months to investigate the market, but finally, our office in Paris could introduce a gentleman who fitted our required profile for employment in Vietnam. Our meeting in a pleasant hotel near the Louvre resulted in an agreement that PG would join us as country representative in Vietnam as soon as possible. PG was originally from Vietnam but got out at an early age to enjoy an education in France, followed by detailed work experience as a logistic forwarder in various parts of the country and Africa. That was just the expertise I had envisaged, and the meeting confirmed that mentally we had a lot in common.

The employment was subject to the approval of the same People's Committee in HCMC, which I had persuaded previously to give permission to Mr Casper to operate in Vietnam. My brain was working overtime when I had to explain the very complex company situation to my dear lady friend in HCMC.

Maybe my frustration and my sincere promises to do well for Vietnam convinced her to get us a new licence for R. I was pleased to convey the good news to PG in Paris. Now we could make final plans for his arrival in Vietnam after the formal documents had been provided. That also meant we would enter the market in Vietnam in direct competition with S, which was not my original intention. Mr Casper understood the reasons, and privately we met as friends whenever I visited Vietnam.

The discussions with PG in Paris did not give him the proper insight into how we could support him once he had established himself as our representative in Vietnam. So we agreed that a few days in our operation in Hong Kong would solve that issue, after which both of us would go to Vietnam for the official introductions to my contacts.

Time was never sufficient, and it was a mad dash to get to Hong Kong Airport on time to catch our flight. One more stop was required on the way, to pick up cash from our bank, which represented the estimated expenses for one month. During a quick transaction at the bank counter, some USD 800.00 were given to me in cash. I just stuffed the money in my pocket, planning to hand it to PG in a safe place without greedy eyes watching us in busy airports.

I remembered my first experience visiting Vietnam, when I instructed PG to declare the USD amount in his immigration arrival form to ensure he would not get picked up for trying to smuggle currency into the country.

On arrival at the airport, I was through the controls in a short time; inverse racism, I suppose? Being Caucasian gave me the fast treatment, whereas PG, although carrying a French passport, was treated like a local citizen returning home. That meant a thorough examination of his belongings, turning out pockets and giving reasons for his visit. It got a little difficult when the border authorities asked him to show the USD 800.00 of cash PG declared on his entry form; that money was still in my pocket while I was waiting outside for my new staff member to appear. After 30 minutes, I realised something was wrong and tried to get back into the immigration hall to explain to the officers that I had forgotten to pass the cash on as intended. Unfortunately, I could not even state my case; I got pushed out into the street again without further explanations. Stupid me, I didn't even think that those control freaks might even have reasons to charge me with the possession of illegal funds when I did not declare the money on my arrival form.

Nearly two hours after arrival, PG finally was released and came out to meet me. He had been accused of false declarations, and his passport was taken away until further investigations could be undertaken. That was not exactly the best welcome home party for a Vietnamese who had not been back to his country since he left for France at 14 years. I apologised for my mistake and promised to do my best to get this sorted out; as to how, I had no idea yet.

Over the next two days, PG had to attend further police interrogations. Finally, I had had enough of the charade and wrote a letter stating the facts of how this situation eventuated and took the entire blame for my action, with an apology added.

PG got his passport back with a warning not to do anything illegal again. A penalty was imposed, which happened to be exactly the amount of USD 800.00, which caused all this commotion. PG was upset and worried about the money, but that was already history. It was my fault, and therefore I would replace the funds so that PG could start his new life back in his home country without further worries on that score.

We did our rounds of official introductions in HCMC and Hanoi; after that, PG was on his own to find a place to stay, settle into the office of our agents and get some business so we could pay for his expenses. That may have been tough, but it was the best therapy to get him to think positively and forget the first few days of returning to his home country.

In our business, communication is the most essential factor. To get results, information, advice, questions and answers need to be handled in the quickest way possible. That was difficult in Vietnam because of the lack of infrastructure. Telephone lines were only available in limited numbers. The Internet may have been invented already, but very few people around the globe understood what that was all about. The only alternative was the fax machine, rated as a high-tech form of communication replacing the cumbersome telex machines. Using the fax sounded good, but the cost was almost prohibitive. A 4-page text sent out of Vietnam by fax would cost USD 20.00, the same for incoming faxes. Phone calls were equally expensive and to be restricted to only the most important occasions; all that did not help a new operation to get started.

However, I encountered similar problems in other Asian countries. Hong Kong was an exception, and the clever people in that place came up with new ideas that used a combination of computers and telephone lines. That innovation originated from the cost-saving method of using telex machines during the off-peak hours by slowing the transmission down to minimum speed and allowing a much higher usage of the cables to overseas destinations.

When computers were first used in offices in Hong Kong, simple software allowed users to prepare messages, like fax. By dialling a telephone number in Hong Kong, they would send their accumulated message to the company computer. The messages would be bundled up and sent overnight at reduced rates to Asia or Europe and delivered by fax. If the receiver had installed the same simple software, he could dial up the Hong Kong number and retrieve and send many messages for the telephone cost of 60 to 90 seconds. So, that's what we did in our office in Vietnam.

Twice a day, PG would call up the computer in Hong Kong and collect our messages and send his own to us. We must have saved thousands of dollars on communication costs, and clients were very happy to get fast replies to their questions.

Considering all customers had similar problems starting up new ventures in Vietnam, they understood and valued our capability to close the gap between the faster-moving business in Europe and the slow development in Vietnam.

This much-overlooked factor, plus footwork and the gift of talking the correct language to customers, in English, Vietnamese, and French, combined with professional attitudes, showed excellent results for PG, which pleased him and showed off well in our coffers in Hong Kong. Why, may you ask? Well, the regulations of how to operate a representative office specifically stated that no commercial transactions were allowed to be conducted by the representative. For that reason, all billing for services rendered was done by our Hong Kong office, and profits were shown in the Hong Kong books. It was all legal and correct as all Vietnam operation expenses were also paid from Hong Kong.

One other factor came into play later: the representative of our sister company S in Vietnam, Mr Casper, had several difficulties with his management in Europe; such as the usual problems of communication, lack of management understanding of the daily problems encountered in a developing country, and some overdue reports from Mr Casper. The management was acting totally unfairly as Mr Casper struggled to keep the business going but at the same time had to deal over two months with his wife in intensive care in the hospital as she had suffered a heart attack. Mr Casper was asked to leave and was not very happy about the prospects of going back to Germany without a job. He asked me for help, I gave my opinions to the CEO in Europe, and Mr Casper was given a less stressful position back in the German organisation to be able to look after his wife.

For PG, that also meant he had the market to himself, at least temporarily. He made the best of it. We got very positive comments from our customers and members of our company worldwide.

In contrast, it always puzzled me to understand how an organised and clever entrepreneur could have a very different private life. PG was not an exception, and I guess it came down to his past. Born an Asian, he adopted the French culture but still was an Asian; very complex.

He had been in a relationship when he lived in France and he had visible proof of this when his son was born. Shortly after, PG moved back to Vietnam, and it was only a few months before he met and married a local lady; she gave birth to a little girl soon after.

The wife was tough but a very clever woman with excellent connections. During the Vietnam War, one of her uncles was part of the Viet Cong operating in South Vietnam. I never found out what he was actually doing, but at one time, he had to hide to avoid capture by the South Vietnam authorities and got sheltered by his niece and her family. When the war ended, this uncle was well-connected in the new government. He could open many doors to her and PG, which obviously helped to further the business.

PG and his family were looking for a place to live.

Rents during that time were expensive because of a lack of suitable accommodation. Our contract with PG stipulated a specific housing allowance, but due to local custom, one had to pay upfront for the total rental period. Looking at the figures, it made little sense to rent. PG was able to find a suitable old house which could serve as his office on the ground floor and his living quarters on the top floor. The price to buy was almost the same as two years' rent, and we got permission from my boss in Germany to proceed with this transaction.

PG now owned a house, we had an office and costs were kept down. We thought we had it all under control and looked forward to expanding our business and making plenty of profits.

There were rumours about new investments in the tourist industry and the construction of a brewery. The latter caught my immediate interest. It was supposed to be coming from Germany, complete with an expert beer brewer with promises of a quality beer. The only beer we had consumed in Vietnam was Heineken from Holland, which gave me quite a headache.

As all the existing hotels had been allowed to deteriorate over many years, the tourist industry was desperate for improvements in the accommodation sector, but there was little or no money for maintenance. One of those places was the historic Metropole Hotel in Hanoi, which had been the top address in town during the years from 1901. Famous people, including Charlie Chaplin, had stayed there, but that did not help it to survive the war years in good shape.

It was all very exciting for us as we could see that our transportation and logistics business expertise could be needed. For that reason, I went on another fact-finding trip to Hanoi to investigate who was doing what and how we could get involved. It was necessary to check on the available infrastructure between the port of Haiphong and the city of Hanoi. I remembered the news reports of years before about the terrible bombing campaign of the American Airforce, which destroyed the port, the roads and many bridges during the war. Even though the war officially ended over 16 years ago, the damage was still evident everywhere.

I needed a car to visit Haiphong, situated around 100 km from Hanoi, to make a route inspection and assess the viability of transporting larger equipment. My kind agent in Hanoi, Mr Ng, was helpful by providing a car and a driver but also cautioned me, as official regulations were strict and foreigners had been warned to adhere to them. Leaving the city area without a government escort was not allowed, and the port of Haiphong was definitely off-limits as it was also a Vietnamese Navy port. Well, I considered the driver as my government escort as he worked for a state-owned enterprise; entering the port of Haiphong was another matter to be considered once we got there.

It was a dull morning when we took off. Once out of the city, the so-called highway deteriorated quickly and became an obstacle course. Potholes could be avoided; medium-sized trucks totally overloaded with basic commodities had to be given the right of way as the road was barely wide enough to let two cars pass. Just as well that there were hardly any cars to be seen. Passing extensive rice fields, we had to avoid the farmers who used the road to dry the harvested rice stems and get the trucks to drive over their crop to separate the rice corns from the branches. The wind did the rest, and farmers would just brush the remaining rice into bags to be taken away. The farmers had no equipment, and considering there was no practical alternative, it was amazing to see how widely this method was applied. We had no choice but to help the farmers too, even if it meant we had to slow down to a crawling pace every time we crunched the crop by driving over it.

Some bridges had to be negotiated. They all had been bombed, but at least one lane was repaired to allow traffic to go over. The only problem was that the same lane allowed trains to cross as the rails were put inside the road tarmac. But since few trains were operating due to a lack of rolling stock and engines, we encountered no problems.

It took us nearly 2½ hours to get to Haiphong. That computes to an average speed of 40 km per hour, all things considered quite acceptable.

Arriving at the gate of Haiphong port, it became clear that I could not have a look around inside. I needed to know what port equipment, cranes and lifts, were available to unload cargo arriving for future projects. Rusty old signs warned that entry was prohibited for any unauthorised person. Taking pictures was strictly forbidden, and my driver got a bit nervous when I asked to get closer.

We drove around a little and found a slight hill nearby that allowed us a glimpse of the port from a distance. It just confirmed what I thought I had not seen in close-up. No cranes on the quay, no movement of lifting equipment to be seen; everything seemed to have been in a time-warp for at least 30 years. Maybe two or three vessels; from a distance, they all looked as if they would become scrap metal the next day.

The day was not a total loss. At least, I could confirm the fact that the existing infrastructure would limit the size and weight of any equipment which engineering companies may want to bring in to start their projects. It also became clear that Vietnam would struggle for many years and needed enormous investment to catch up with the western world.

Arriving back in Hanoi late afternoon, I decided to go for a little stroll along the Hoan Kiem Lake (Lake of the Returned Sword) in the city centre to relax and find out what the locals do if they are not working. That task proved difficult as everybody seemed to do something, although I often could not figure out what. Only the little children were playing in the street. Seeing this foreigner hanging around the lakeside, they became quite curious. I had bought one of those half baguettes the Vietnamese have so cleverly adapted from the days of their French colonial occupation. The crispy crust and soft interior were perfect, and I sat on a little stone next to the lake to enjoy it. The young boys got bolder and babbled away, trying to engage me in a conversation. It was all charming, but I could not understand a word as they did not speak English.

They also were very clever. They all tried their best to distract me so I would not notice one young fellow trying to unzip the little bag I carried around. I was thankful for faulty zippers that afternoon. It got stuck a little; I felt the tug and tried to grab my little friend, but to no avail. These guys were skinny and agile, they jumped away and had a big laugh; it was actually very friendly and who is to blame them for trying their skills once every so often?

When talking to various people during my travels, I heard about the days when many Russians were stationed in North Vietnam after the war. Their families escaped Hanoi's summer heat and humidity by staying for up to two months in a mountain resort some two hours' drive from the city. Nobody could tell me if it was still operating, and no information was found anywhere. That intrigued me as it could be another future development project.

However, my driver knew of the place and off we went. This part of the country was quite a contrast to the Eastern area towards Haiphong. Here, there was green vegetation and some forest once we climbed higher into the mountain area where the temperature was much cooler, making it more comfortable for families to stay during the summer months.

We arrived at a hilly settlement with several larger dwellings which could pass as hotels. Some broken down, some boarded up, the whole place looked deserted. I could not see the attraction of anybody wanting to stay there; it all looked grey and miserable. When I get a little depressed, I need some food and a beer; in this place, I needed it badly. We searched some roads up and down and finally found a little business which looked like a small café offering some noodle soup. That was just right for me, and I invited the driver to join me as I could order nothing unless I saw it in front of me.

The place was almost dark inside. It held maybe three or four small tables with rickety chairs to give the weary traveller a chance to relax. We could see nobody at first until a curtain on the end of the dark room opened, and a youngish-looking woman asked us for our order. The noodle soup was OK, beer not, at least that was what I understood. The curtain moved again when two young kids peered at us from what seemed to be the kitchen. There was not another soul in sight, but at least we had a promise of getting a warm noodle soup to cheer us up. But before we could enjoy the meal, a man entered from the street, which turned out to be our host's husband. He seemed to scold his wife for not having provided a lit candle so that we could better see our food. He spoke limited English, but it was enough for me to enquire what he was doing in the settlement. The explanation was that he came back from East Germany after losing his job as a qualified motor mechanic. After East Germany had collapsed and was to be reunited with West Germany, all foreigners employed in the East had to leave as their working visa was not recognised anymore. When I realised this gentleman spent over three years working in Germany, I continued my discussion in German, which he had mastered far better than English. This brought up the subject of beer, and he apologised for not having stock in his little place; but he immediately left to return with some warm beer he must have purchased somewhere nearby. I declined the offer of ice cubes to cool down my beer as you never know where the water comes from in those parts of the world.

We had a great conversation, and he was happy to mention that he had found a job in this little village delivering the few items of mail every week to the remaining residents. The resort had been shut for many years. However, the locals stayed on because jobs elsewhere were also not available.

We had to depart and received the friendly invitation to come back again soon. Many other priorities existed in the country before such a place could be rebuilt. It would take years before the emerging tourists would venture out of the cities to enjoy the fresh mountain air.

I did not know the place and still can't remember the name or the area; I just had crossed it off my priorities list as too hard and too long to eventuate.

⌒

There was one charming aspect of visiting Hanoi. PG introduced me to a couple of artists who had studied at the local university and had become well known as accomplished painters. Mai Hien Bui initially created eggshell paintings, whereas her husband, Dao Anh Khanh did some very distinctive work in oil with country scenes evoking local folklore. Their little studio, close to the diplomatic area in Hanoi, was a small house where the couple lived downstairs and worked upstairs under the roof with illumination coming from a skylight. Getting to the studio involved climbing a steep ladder and holding on to a thick rope for support.

I visited several times, looked at their recent work, shared some tea with them and bought a few paintings. A friend in Sydney liked them and asked me to buy a couple for her as well; I became a good customer of the artists.

To say the least, Mai's husband differed from what I would have expected but then again, what did I expect of a talented Vietnamese artist? I really don't know. Our discussions, in halting English, always ended up in talks about the music that he loved but was limited to what was then considered appropriate to Vietnamese culture; no western-style music was condoned in the country for a long time. Although I witnessed the first changes in 1989 in HCMC, Hanoi's very strict and communist city did not catch up until much later.

I invited the family, including their little daughter, Jenny, to a French restaurant operated in a small townhouse on Saturday. The owner, cook and host was a doctor of medicine who had followed his passion for French cuisine in his later years and provided a delicious meal. After a sumptuous dinner, we all went to my hotel, the Thang Loi, which held a dance night featuring a live band with some noisy, western-style music every Saturday night. It was ladies' night, and they were allowed in free. We all hopped around together, and the little girl joined in with enthusiasm, although she was still too small and had to be carried in our arms most of the time. It was not long before Mai's husband started displaying a dance style that I had not seen before. Happy on his own, he jumped around and appeared to have great fun. I suppose there was some rum involved, but I was not sure. We had a great time. The band comprised local amateurs but included that German gentleman who was employed by the East German Embassy in Hanoi.

Sometime later, when I revisited their studio, Khanh proudly announced that he had discovered Space music, whatever that was. I admit to being pretty ignorant about that sort of thing. The visible result of his recovery was the style of oil paintings he produced; gone were the sedate and countrified pictures of the past. He now used plenty of colours, abstract themes and new signature items which appeared in all of his latest paintings. One was a hidden fish eye somewhere on the canvas, and the other was just the tuning bar of an old native string instrument, the *Dan Nhi*, a two-string fiddle.

I am still comparing these two styles of paintings in my home, trying to understand the complete transformation which took place in the artist's head.

Sadly, on one of my last trips to Hanoi, I found that there had been other changes. The couple had split up; Mai stayed in their old studio as Khanh moved further out of the city and opened his own place. Both continued to work with outstanding success, getting international recognition through exhibitions in the USA and Europe.

Back to the harsh world of business.

My situation in Hong Kong became tight. The merger between the two companies would take place very soon. It was logical that our organisation, having a much smaller overseas representation, would be incorporated into S worldwide. The ugly fact of synergy effects stared us in the face. Some departments would be closed, and others would be merged with the larger network. That meant we had to give notice to 70 per cent of our staff in Hong Kong, and PG in Vietnam was to be integrated with S in HCMC. PG was unhappy, but I persuaded him to go along for a year to see what opportunities might come up. He could still make up his own mind.

My staff in Hong Kong got some compensation and found jobs, and I was relieved it worked out reasonably well.

My situation was different; there was no room for two top people in Hong Kong; I was offered the choice to take over Vietnam, pick one region in the USA or go to Indonesia. Well, Indonesia was for me, which meant I inherited enough problems to worry about and could not get further involved in Vietnam. PG stayed with the company for one year and started his own business, being a very clever and hardworking expert. There was nothing much I could do in support anyway, so we kept in touch purely on a personal basis.

The USA finally normalised their relationship with Vietnam in 1995.

Translated, that meant they now wanted to earn money for what they delivered to the country. The bombs they dropped 20 years earlier, during the war were only paid for by the American taxpayers; now, it seemed to be the right time to cash in on the developing economy of Vietnam.

As I said earlier, that is the harsh world of doing business.

It took a long time to plan, but finally, I managed to revisit Indochina, this time purely as a tourist.

Fast Forward to the Year 2012

My wife, Rosita, and I flew to Siem Reap in Cambodia to visit the ancient ruins of Angkor Wat. Arriving at Siem Reap Airport brought back memories of several arrivals in Vietnam many years ago. Elementary facilities, hardly any air-conditioning and similar bureaucratic procedures to enter the country. The only remarkable difference was the smiling face of the immigration officer and his open invitation to let him have some money since he was kind enough to process our e-visa without fuss. That kind of behaviour would have been unheard of in Vietnam, but I must admit it was a more pleasant way to enter a country.

After the mandatory sightseeing had been dealt with we went into the little town centre to find out what made this place tick. A local market was an eye-opener. The myriad items on offer at very low prices were most likely counterfeits from China or India. It was a very interesting excursion, but a hot and sticky experience, and the temperature and humidity made it almost compulsory to find a place offering a cool beer.

There were no shortages of little bars; in fact, one street was actually called Bar Street. Most offered happy hour prices, and most were owned by foreigners; listening to them talking, it became apparent that the majority came from Australia.

Our hotel was the meeting point of the tour group who would join us on a trip down the Mekong River. First, we had to take a bus to a boarding place next to the Tonle Sap Lake to be transferred to several small powerboats to join the vessel. Our river boat awaited us in the middle of the lake. We clambered on board with little time to spare before a violent rainstorm engulfed us in sheets of water. We were wet but happy to be safely on board. Finally, we were shown to our comfortable cabins to begin our seven-night journey toward the Mekong Delta and Saigon.

We visited some villages along the river and spent almost a day wandering around Phnom Penh, the capital of Cambodia. The next day we were supposed to enter Vietnam. Vivid memories of my previous visits conjured up images of keen Vietnam customs officers coming on board, checking every document, comparing faces on the passport with the person depicted and getting lots of questions about who we are and what we intend to do in Vietnam. The actual crossing into Vietnam from Cambodia was done by floating on our riverboat down the Mekong at a slow pace. During that time, some crew members visited the Cambodian and Vietnamese border stations we could see on the riverside. They all looked very ordinary, a small house with a big flag pole standing next to it. The Cambodian and Vietnamese flags made it clear who represented whom. I was just relieved that procedures had become so easy for tourists during the last 15 years; I could just sit on the deck, enjoy a cool beer and cross an almost invisible border marked only by a couple of flag posts. That's the way I like it!

The tour organiser had done a great job. They made arrangements with a few villages along the river to accept visitors into their community to experience how the people in the country live. The villages got some financial assistance for their community projects in exchange for opening their places to strangers who would be welcomed but not accosted on every corner to buy some trinkets. The visits included an orphanage, a Buddhist school and some home visits where we met with students specially selected to further their English studies by practicing their skills during talks with the foreign visitors. That was all very pleasant, and we all felt that the people were warm and friendly. I was sure that this would also reflect in the minds of members of our group when returning home to their countries and meeting Vietnamese people who are trying to integrate into a strange culture.

It was almost a sad moment when we disembarked in a small town to be taken by a modern bus from the Mekong Delta to HCMC, which was only about 70 km away. An official tour included another two days of visiting various places in and around HCMC, all of which I still could remember clearly. They included the Carlton Hotel, the Ritz Hotel, the Opera, the City of HCMC Town Hall, and the Independence Palace. The only noticeable difference was that all buildings and streets had been cleaned and looked in good repair.

It is almost compulsory to visit the Cu Chi Tunnels outside HCMC. It was almost a disappointment as the place had become such a tourist attraction that very few of the original sites were recognisable. The official purpose was to act as a memorial to the deeds of the Viet Cong during the war, but to me, it appeared to be a tourist trap just to make money.

Another visit was fascinating as I could not get close to the Independence Palace on my previous visits to HCMC. That building was the seat of the South Vietnamese government. It became famous for a picture showing a North Vietnamese tank pushing through the front gate to allow the soldiers to storm in and take over the grounds to symbolise the ultimate defeat of South Vietnam. Now we were allowed inside; it was all spick and span; the most interesting room was the conference room, nicely set up to show where many important decisions had been made, which most likely cost millions of people immense hardship or even their lives.

We extended our stay in HCMC after the official tour was finished. After so many years, I contacted PG, and we met at our hotel. Lunch was in order, and I asked to be taken back to my favourite noodle place in Rue Pasteur. Sure enough, it still existed. Nothing much had changed. A full house, noise, steaming bowls of *Pho* being dished up in large quantities, a culinary delight which had guests coming for many years. What better proof of a quality restaurant can you get?

We had lots of years to catch up with. PG had many health issues but kept his business growing with the help of his son, Marc. Many years before, I met Marc when he was studying in Perth. We were invited to a BBQ for friends in Kings Park and invited Marc even though I had never met him before. He arrived all dressed up in a suit, strutting around the park with a good-looking young lady on his arm. He was a little out of place at a BBQ in his outfit, but the story came out that he wanted to quit university and become a model. Well, he had the looks and was pretty tall; the good-looking lady accompanying him was a model from the Philippines. That most likely was the primary incentive to switch from studying to modelling.

PG was not impressed by this new idea and somehow got Marc to finish his study and join his business in HCMC.

On further questioning about what happened to PG in the intervening years, some more interesting stories emerged. Marc was the first issue of an earlier liaison with a French lady in France. When PG came to HCMC, he married a local Vietnamese and had a daughter. In between the years, I lost track of things and found out only during lunch that PG had another wife now who had given him another son. That was a lot to absorb in a short time, but it all fell into place when we visited the office of PG, somewhere between the city and the port. A large, sensible, square building with warehouse space on the ground and a couple of floors with office space for the company and some extra rooms to be let out to other parties. The top floor was converted into a vast apartment where PG and his new family lived. Their little boy could drive around the spacious rooms on a little tricycle; the flat was bright, with a sweeping view over flat land towards the harbour.

Business obviously had been good to PG, but he lived a simple life. When inspecting his warehouse, I noticed a large Mercedes car parked in the middle. It turned out to belong to PG, but he would not use it in HCMC. He had picked us up in town in a simple Japanese SUV, unremarkable and one of many on the roads.

PG had to admit on questioning him that things were difficult in Vietnam. With corruption, competition, and official red tape, he felt he had to fly below the radar to continue business without calling attention to himself. But one thing became clear. PG had taken responsibility for his offspring without hesitation. Marc was a director in his company, in charge of sales and communication. His daughter was just old enough to have been sent to England for a college education. His youngest son was still attached to the proverbial apron of the mother but no doubt would receive a worthwhile education in due time.

I was happy to have met PG again, that things seemed to go well for him, although his health had to be taken care of. We promised to stay in touch and departed for Hanoi for another few days of playing tourist.

My wife, Rosita, had never been to Vietnam before, so I had to ensure we ticked off all the important sites according to the guidebooks. One highlight was supposed to be a visit to the Mausoleum to pay homage to Ho Chi Minh, locally known as Uncle Ho. It was not to be. The Mausoleum was closed, and although no official notification was given, rumours clearly suggested that the body had been shipped to Moscow to be embalmed again as it needed to be done every few years. This was not possible in Vietnam, and Russian know-how was required. After all, they had plenty of experience doing the same to the body of Lenin, who had been on display for many years in Moscow.

An overnight trip with a boat on Ha Long Bay was praised as the most romantic highlight when visiting Hanoi. There were spectacular views and lovely boats; unfortunately, far too many of those were full of noisy Koreans and Chinese tourists who seemed to party all night. I could not get away from there fast enough.

We stayed in the Hilton Hotel near the Opera as part of the package. It did not exist on my last visit so many years ago, but since the USA had opened the relationship with Vietnam again, many investments have been made. When visiting the Thang Loi Hotel for nostalgic reasons, I was happy that not much had changed except for a general overhaul and paint job. Some villas had been added along the lakeside to accommodate longer staying guests. A road leading to the hotel had been lined with more expensive-looking houses. The entire area had a feeling of affluent suburbia.

One last important visit was to the studio of Mai Hien Bui. The sign outside was still the same, although the name of Khanh was hard to read as it was not repainted during the last renovation.

Mai Hien was there, and it took a few moments before she remembered our old acquaintance. She looked a bit worn out, older, of course, and it transpired that she had had a traffic accident some time ago, which left her with some unpleasant side effects. Working with acrylics was not good for her health because of the fumes, and she intended to switch entirely to painting with oils on canvas. It was sad to see, as she had been, or still was, the best known acrylic painter in Vietnam and overseas. She even sold a picture to the then American Secretary of State, Hillary Clinton, and proudly displayed a picture of that event on her studio wall. Maybe one of the last acrylic pictures created by Mai was sold to a keen admirer. To my wife! Again, the moment was immortalised with photos being taken, and it was a happy occasion for all concerned. Maybe I have to mention that my wife has been painting for many years. The discussion with Mai obviously concentrated on their art, which left me out in the cold; I am pretty ignorant of the finer points of painting.

When asking about her daughter, Jenny, Mai informed us she was studying in the USA; I can't remember what subjects she mentioned.

There was no time left to make it out of the city to visit the new studio of Dao Anh Khanh. I noted it down for the next visit to Hanoi, whenever that may be.

When checking recently, I found out that Khanh is running a little accommodation business alongside his studio. His daughter Jenny seems to help or running the business, including the art gallery.

It has been many years that I have been involved, on and off, with Vietnam and the last trip reconfirmed that I still like the country, the people and the food. We are fortunate that we can meet the people and enjoy Vietnamese food in Australia, but the fascinating country of Vietnam has to be experienced firsthand. I must arrange my travel calendar soon to squeeze in another visit to Vietnam.

Retirement makes you do strange things. For instance, you become interested in improving your survivalist cooking style, and baking bread; you try revisiting your roots in your native Berlin, Germany. What a change to the 27 hectic and challenging years working as an executive in Asia.

Retirement Fun

For years my wife Rosita and I had contemplated an extended trip to my home city of Berlin, which I left behind 56 years ago when my life as a gipsy began.

In the intervening years, brief business trips home whetted my appetite to spend more time in that vibrant city.

Our original plan, to rent an apartment for three months, changed after the 2016 terrorist attacks took place, right in the centre of the main Berlin shopping area. (My wife strongly believes that her name is on top of the list whenever, or wherever, another attack takes place.) OK, a compromise was agreed upon, and we finally booked a small apartment in what they call *Berlin-Mitte*. That means Berlin Centre. I did not initially realise that, before East and West Berlin were reunited, the area had belonged to East Berlin. Since 1953, West Berliners could not travel freely to the other side of the wall in East Berlin; that area of the city was not part of my world when I was growing up, leaving a white blotch on my mental map of Berlin.

Regardless, we set off, driving on the *autobahn* from Frankfurt north to Berlin, and passed through the old East Germany via Weimar and Erfurt – where Martin Luther proclaimed his split from the doctrines of the Catholic Church in 1493 – historically very interesting but hardly relevant in today's fast-living society.

However, before 1989, on coming closer to Berlin, we would have been looking for signs of the next East German checkpoint, manned by those dreaded uniformed men posted there from the province of Saxony.

This was done to make sure that the checkpoints would not become a friendly meeting point between the citizens of the town, albeit from the other side of the wall. To make the division even more apparent, these strangers at the gates spoke a strong German dialect (from Saxony), a dialect that became very much disliked and associated with the Communist regime.

The 2017 sun was now shining, and even though the traffic is horrendous, the fact that no borders had to be crossed was an enormous relief.

The apartment was OK, and the transport system in Berlin is fantastic. Not being able to find a reasonably priced car park for the next four weeks, we returned the rented car. A monthly public transportation network ticket would serve us perfectly to get around on the underground, bus, tram and city train services.

I had strange feelings and was wary about our neighbourhood; there were more pubs and cafés than ever before. Foreign tongues could be heard everywhere, and it was quite difficult to find a local person to communicate with.

A friend from past days in Indonesia had started a bakery, well-known in one part of town. He was proud to produce excellent sourdough bread. He offered to give me a 'shot-gun apprenticeship' to learn a few tricks of the trade. I had fiddled around at home for a while, but my finished product was never up to standard, so I jumped at the opportunity.

We started on a Sunday afternoon; I mixed the sourdough starter with flour and water. When the dough looked and felt right, it had to be folded seven times every 30 minutes. It was a good reminder that working as a baker would never suit an old man; I could not lift the 10 kg trays to higher levels anymore.

Overnight storing in the fridge caused the dough to rise even more. Monday morning, it had to be divided into smaller portions to form the bread shape and let it rise further to the desired level. It was exciting to wait for the final inspection of the bread after baking. The freshly baked bread smelt mouth-wateringly delicious on opening the oven, and I couldn't wait to taste it. Tapping the bread, it sounded hollow. Cut it, and the inside showed holes in the texture, which shows the natural yeast of the sourdough had done its job. Finally, the eating test. It was scrumptious, with a hint, but not too strong, of a sour taste. I finally graduated with honours after two days of hard work.

Being in a central location made it easier for friends to find excuses to visit us in Berlin. It seems that the attraction of the Metropole for home-grown Germans has not diminished over the years – food galore, pubs galore, tourists galore. The latter part finally got on my nerves, and it was clear that this sort of sharing of my home town with an overwhelming number of foreigners would not sit well with me in the long run. However, being tourists ourselves, at least for a short duration, the transport ticket was used extensively. We had already got our money's worth within the first two weeks.

We targeted and visited any place on the map that was unfamiliar to me because of the past East-West division. There was a whole new world out there, making me realise how limited we, West Berliners, really were during the division of our city and how complicated it had been to travel through East Germany to get to anywhere outside.

We were not into accumulating souvenirs during the trip. Still, I could not help gaining some 4 kg of extra weight due to the extended foodie excursions – it was not necessarily gourmet cooking in most places, but it was tasty. The beer just goes too well with that kind of food.

Tired but inspired, we ended our trip after 70 days abroad. Now we had another task: to find the right equipment and ingredients to suit our home-baking and cooking capabilities and emulate the treats we had overseas.

It was back to retirement fun.

> No, this is not another story by Jules Verne, although it could have happened in his rich imagination.

Journey to the Interior

It all started as a routine. Coming to a certain age, the local authorities require a medical examination of any applicant wanting to renew his driver's licence. No problem for me, as I felt fit and alert with the help of my trusted CPAP (Continuous Positive Airway Pressure – breathing help for *apnea*) machine. As part of the examination, a urine test was required to ensure I was not indulging in drug orgies, which might impair my ability to negotiate public roads when driving. Again, there was no issue with that, as I live a relatively clean life – if I do not mention my love of wines and the occasional dram of whisky. My request to extend my driver's licence was granted without further problem.

But here is where the story goes in a different direction. My diligent GP pointed out that they had found a minute amount of blood in my specimen and suggested consulting with a specialist to determine if I was suffering from cancer in my bladder or elsewhere.

I am a doubting cynic who always suspects that somebody is trying to take advantage of me. My GP and I have a special relationship, in so far as he will try his best to keep me alive to ensure his future income will not stop with my demise. On the other hand, I have been happy to go along with his health care as being alive gives me the chance to acknowledge that the money is well spent. We are therefore walking on common ground; it is a win-win situation.

Consequently, I followed my GP's advice and consulted with the specialist in his rooms. A tiny reception area and a larger waiting room with several sick-looking people waiting for whatever news they would get.

When it was my turn, the doctor called me in. It was very spacious, elegantly furnished, and had a splendid view over the Swan River. All my years in business, I never had such a friendly office as a managing director in various companies and countries where I had to work. The doctor was dressed in a black shirt and pants, his hair smoothly groomed over his head and ears. A friendly introduction was followed by a computer illustration of what a human body contains and which parts he specialised in. A concise description of his planned action ensued, which gave me a slight hint that something strange would happen to me soon. With the help of his reception, I made an appointment for a future date on which I needed to present myself to the hospital where the doctor practised his art.

The day had come. I blocked out almost every thought on how and what could happen and drove to the hospital very early in the morning. I had been told the whole procedure would only take one hour, and after that, I could drive home with no problem. That indicated that any anaesthetics would only be applied locally and that I would be wide awake to watch the action.

I am not very good at hospitals. The whole routine of checking in and changing my clothes with those ridiculously complicated hospital gowns put me on edge. After that, I was ushered through half the building to get to the operating theatre to meet the man who had my fortune in his hands.

Two friendly nurses, well past their blushing ages, greeted me and led me to a surgery bed in the centre of the room. There was my specialist doctor, waiting with a friendly smile and greeting. This time he was more casually dressed, in a white open-neck shirt, arms slightly exposed. The combination with the black trousers made him look like a matador ready to spar with the wild bull in the ring. There was one significant difference. The doctor did not hold a sword in his rubber-gloved hands but a little gadget that looked like a joystick ready to be used in a computer game.

The entrance to my urinary tract was exposed, an anaesthetic gel was applied, and an extra pillow was pushed under my head to make it more comfortable to watch a tiny colour TV screen. Let the journey begin.

I had been warned that I might experience strange feelings when a tiny camera was pushed down the urinary tract. The first reaction was the unreasonable urge to revisit the bathroom, although I just had emptied my bladder minutes before. Next, I viewed a long tunnel in reddish-brown colours, which seemed to lead into the depth of my body. The doctor manipulated the little camera slowly inside the urinary tract and gave his comments on what we saw, like a well-trained tour guide. After what seemed to be a long distance, we had a brief stop when the prostate gland came into sight. The assessment of what the doctor saw was definitely very positive (in a good sense). On we went down the tube until we came into a small cave which displayed a warm, friendly picture. The colour of the walls was almost ochre, with lots of thin red lines on the sides. The tranquil picture quickly changed when bubbles appeared, which blurred the vision and ruined the image. My tour guide explained he had just injected some water down the tube to enlarge the cave to have a better look at what he described as my bladder. I had to believe him for lack of any other explanation. His action showed a remarkable ballooning of the cave to allow the camera to expose all parts to be examined in detail. The conclusion was that the excursion proved to very successful. No faults in the structure or rendering had been observed, and the camera was retrieved from the tunnel by the very experienced doctor. At one point, I nearly suggested that he would qualify as a drone pilot in any organisation, but I kept my mouth shut as I was still exposed to the world and did not want to appear ungrateful for what he had achieved.

Retreating to the change room, I had to make a quick pit-stop in the bathroom to ensure I was not bursting. Regardless of that action, I was also very relieved about the results, as the idea of having to pay another visit for a surgical procedure did not sit well with me. It turned out all good in the end.

Curiosity got the better of me. I had to find out what my learned tour guide had called this procedure in his language. It turned out to be 'Flexible Cystoscopy'. Surprisingly, the basic instrument and Cystoscopy procedure were invented by a German Army surgeon, Dr Philipp Bonzini, who wanted to trace bullets in his patients' bodies after they were shot. The year was 1807. That means Jules Verne could have written one of his fascinating stories on that subject, but to my knowledge, he never did.

To most humans, seeing birds in flight is a regular occurrence; after all, that is what birds do.

Then some people developed a fascination with the idea of flying and pondered why and how birds can fly. Early experiments emulating birds often ended in tragedy, but did not discourage others from taking the next steps to achieve their goal.

It took over a century to develop workable flying machines to allow a man to join birds in the sky. The powerful flapping of a bird's wings could not be duplicated and got replaced by a fixed structure incorporating some of the aerodynamics observed in birds in flight. Engines driving propellers pulled the machine forward, and the resulting airflow over the unique curved surface of the fixed-wing created sufficient lift to get airborne. Man finally followed his dream to fly.

The Dream to Fly

Too young to understand all this, my first encounter with airplanes created fear and total distrust of anything that flew. The first sign that something bad was happening came from an ear-splitting sound of sirens warning about squadrons of heavy airplanes approaching our city of Berlin to drop their bombs. A scramble of mothers and children into the cellar followed, and the anxious wait began. When the bombs landed nearby with a terrifying bang, a pressure wave shook the building, and it took quite a while before the dust settled again. Only when the sirens sounded the all-clear could we get out of the cellar and try to figure out what had happened. We saw the destruction of trees and houses around us, maybe small sheets of aluminium foil tumbling out of the sky. That was the final farewell of the departing airplanes as they tried to obscure their image on the ground radar screens tracking them.

I cannot recall seeing the beauty of a bird in flight, and the planes represent something we feared and despised instead. At the age of four, one does not understand the world well and is guided by the reactions of the adults who formed our world.

It took over three years until my feelings for airplanes changed.

Political games of the powers in charge resulted in the blockade of that part of Berlin, controlled by the Western Allies. No movements of goods by truck, rail or inland water transport was allowed. This was in fact an attempt to starve the city and force a total surrender of nearly two million people. The only access was the open-air corridor, to allow planes to fly in and out of the city.

A group of clever people put their heads together and created the plan to build an air bridge by using every available airplane to fly to Berlin to provide essentials for the citizen's survival. Most of the vegetables had to be de-hydrated to save weight and make them last longer, and the potatoes and milk came in powder form to be reconstituted at the destination.

Around two-thirds of the total cargo volume was represented by coal, needed to produce electricity on a minimal scale in the city. Three airports opened in Berlin to allow planes to land every three minutes to offload their cargo and turn around quickly to get more supplies. Over 2.3 million tons of freight were flown into the besieged city by over 270,000 flights.

We boys got to know the sound of the different aircraft engines and realised that this time those planes were bringing something good to the city instead of bombs. It became a regular occurrence that pilots flying overhead dropped small packets out of their cockpit to the joy of the children, who found a few sweet delights on the ground. We renamed the planes, calling them *Rosinenbomber,* meaning 'Raisin Bombers'.

The operation of the air bridge carried on from June 1948 until September 1949, when the Russians finally realised that their plan had not worked. After that, the borders opened again for transport, and the city of Berlin began a slow recovery, which took many years.

It is not surprising that the experience of seeing and hearing aircraft flying over our heads every three minutes had an impact on me. The pilots of those planes became heroes to us, even though dark memories of the war lingered in the back of my mind; I wanted to become a pilot myself.

Dreaming, we became hotshot pilots by folding and gluing paper into shapes. Competitions of whose contraption stayed airborne the longest or how far and straight these simple devices travelled kept our interest high for a long time. No other opportunity to experience flight presented itself to us for many years after the blockade.

West Berlin was still a political island in the middle of East Germany, administered by the four Allied Powers, with a revolving command every thirty days. The economic recovery took time, and there was zero chance to look at any aviation sport in that city.

Somehow the daily drudgery of school almost squashed any fancy idea of becoming a pilot. After graduating high school with mediocre results, I tried to get into Lufthansa German Airlines to be trained as a pilot. Not having achieved matriculation, that door closed. I needed to explore another avenue. Since Berlin still had a special status, there was no army or air force to join, but this left open a possible move to West Germany, where I could apply to an organisation to give me the flight training.

My sins from the past finally caught up with me; I think that's when I regretted having been a lazy student in school. I hardly ever did my homework. As a result, the exam results did not qualify me to join any flying circus, and forget about formal training organisations.

Necessity forced me to look for other avenues to earn a living. I became what I call a pen-pusher after finishing an apprenticeship with a transport company. At least I got some excitement moving cargo around the world, although my involvement with the work mostly involved paperwork.

Somehow I needed more appreciation, and I took a position in Switzerland and the UK to gain more experience. It also got me closer to airplanes as the work involved dispatching cargo by air freight to worldwide destinations. It still needed paperwork, but at least I could watch these take-offs and landings when working at the airports of Basel, Zurich and London Heathrow. London proved outright exciting. I had never flown, but sitting in the grass less than 100 metres from the runway gave me an experience that was as close as possible. British Airways tested their brand new Comet passenger jet by doing circuit training. On take-off, I got blasted with hot, smelly exhaust fumes. The dust on the tarmac and the cut grass muddied my sandwich, which I consumed during lunch hour. That presented excitement enough to temporarily satisfy my dream to become a pilot.

I still sometimes scratch my head in wonder at how lax security around the airport must have been; curious folk (like me, say) wandering onto the tarmac were not restrained by a fence or other security system.

In London, I made friends with several Australians. I listened with intense interest to their talk about their country, the culture of the Indigenous people and the wide-open space awaiting them on their return. Fascinating stuff for a young fellow full of desires to see the world and do something different from his routine.

The vital question was how to get there. Alan, one of my Australian friends, decided to return by driving overland as far as possible before taking a ship for the final leg of the journey. I got hooked and asked if I could join him on the trip. He accepted the idea happily; sharing expenses and experiences provided a strong motivation.

As a result, I had to go back to Switzerland to earn more money to make this trip a reality.

Working at Zurich airport, I got very close to airplanes, although only on the outside. As transport agents, we had to attend to some exceptional tasks that required us to actually supervise the loading of the cargo into the aircraft parked on the tarmac. How exciting to be able to actually touch an aircraft. The cargoes did not always offer happiness; we had to, for instance, organise flights for a deceased Jewish person who wanted to be buried in Israel.

Other times it was a relief to put the cargo onto the airplane as we finally parted with slightly more dangerous cargo. Dangerous because of the nature of the goods: Banknotes and coins. We had a couple of banks in Zurich as clients. Frequently they had to airfreight cash currencies back to various countries, and our job involved picking up the boxes from the underground loading bay near the vaults and delivering them directly to the airport. One condition imposed by the insurance company was that a Swiss National had to carry a weapon to satisfy the security conditions required on those transports in a private vehicle. As a non-Swiss, I did not qualify but I am happy to confirm that my Swiss counterpart had the sense to put the gun in plain sight on the back seat. So in case of any hold-up, he intended to point that out to any villain; they could take the cash, but we might not be physically harmed.

My time in Switzerland came to an end, and a new world opened for me on arrival in Sydney, Australia, in January 1966.

My first priority was to find a job to keep myself fed and housed. Any dreams of flying evaporated quickly when I was employed as a labourer with the Sydney Water Board to dig trenches with a jackhammer and shovel to facilitate the laying of sewage pipes to service the new suburban areas.

After a couple of months, I got a position with Qantas, the Australian Airlines. Any hope of even spotting an aircraft diminished when I got introduced to the actual work. It turned out to be just mind-numbing; sharing an office with eight other enslaved people, we had to pick up an enormous bunch of copy airline tickets and write the three-letter IATA airport code against each port the ticket had been issued to. Another group of people would then punch these codes into a vast computer to record what portion of the fares would be allocated to partner airlines. My past expertise in airport codes worldwide became handy, but that was not how I wanted to end my youthful dreams. In hindsight, I can only say that the powers in charge in Qantas missed out on getting a clever young man to become a loyal and productive member of the staff by not employing my talents in more suitable areas. So there we are, I said it.

I survived three months in that job, and was ready to return to Europe,

The mood changed to elation when I finally got back into my profession. The company I trained with in Germany had a tiny branch in Sydney and employed me to knock on doors to drum up new business. Today you would call that a Business Development Manager. In that capacity, I had much to do with airlines. As a result, an invitation arrived for our company/me to join a training class for six days in Hamburg, Germany; it changed my life, it was actually too good to be true. I had to digest the news first, I did not believe it; this would mean I actually would fly in an airplane for the first time in my life.

A group of us boarded the Boeing 707 four-engine jet in Sydney for the long journey to Germany. We had four stops to refuel and drop off or pick up new passengers, which opened up a whole new world for me. Each time we landed, I shivered with excitement. How such a giant metal tube with engines managed to decent smoothly enough to touch down on the tarmac at high speed and only then put the powerful engines into reverse thrust to slow down sufficiently to taxi safely to the arrival building. Even on approaching the airport in a different country, one could find a distinct smell in the air, promising a different world. Part of that world would join us when new passengers boarded the plane for the next part of the journey. People with varying clothing, colour and smells made an exciting mix I found fascinating. To round off the experience, I tasted the food served to the newcomers, which included many delicious titbits originating in the country we had just left behind. I experienced the exotic differences between Singapore, Bombay, Abu Dhabi, and Athens on the one flight before landing in Germany.

During the long flight at night, I hardly slept, and that is where I saw another strange thing. The plane had a glass bubble on top of the fuselage, which looked odd. But then, I saw the co-pilot or navigator climbing a short ladder positioned below this bubble in the middle of the night. He actually took a shot at the clear sky to confirm the aircraft's geographical position and place. Do not think of a shot in the ordinary sense; I had seen it before on ships when the experts used a sextant to 'shoot the stars' to reassure the master that their calculations of time, speed and geographical position proved correct.

This all happened in an airplane flying several 1,000 feet in the air. Why did they do that? It all came down to the fact that today's GPS (Global Positioning System) did not exist. Pilots and crew had their gyrocompass. They had maps and accurate time measuring pieces to calculate their route, but there was always a chance that head or tailwinds might make a mockery of their mathematical abilities. That is how the navigator explained this strange happening to me that night. I admit I had no idea what he was talking about, and it took several years before it all became clear.

The return journey turned out even more exciting; we stopped off in Istanbul, Beirut, Abu Dhabi and Saigon before I had to change planes in Hong Kong for my last leg to Sydney. I totally enjoyed flying, but it was time to get back to the reality of the daily task on hand.

Three years later, my fortunes changed with a transfer to the (then) backwaters of Perth, WA, to open a small branch office for the company. This journey did not involve any flying as I had to complete the 4,000 plus km trip by car, to carry my sparse belongings to my new destination. The only excitement on that trip was the long stretch of unpaved road through the Nullarbor, providing ample opportunities for accidents or getting stuck in mud holes after a downpour. A thought came to mind that flying would have been so much more elegant.

My first months in Perth turned out be rather harsh. Our tiny apartment in Fremantle faced west, and the sun heated the bricks on the little balcony so much that frying an egg seemed to be no problem. With no air-conditioning one had to open the front door, barricade it with a chair to prevent anybody from walking in and do the same on the balcony to get some airflow going.

The first office in Fremantle was 18 miles from the airport, which meant long drives daily to attend to business. My VW Kombi Wagon never cooled down, and often, I burned my hands on the steering wheel after parking somewhere in the sun for a while. Official business attire meant shorts, long socks, a short-sleeved shirt and a tie around the neck. Even the bank clerks followed this fashion as it would have been unbearable to sit in the stifling hot offices all day clad in a suit.

It took almost a year before I got a little office in the aircraft hangar of Ansett Australia Airlines. The few airplanes taking off or landing made plenty of noise but we could not see them from the single window in our office, which faced away from the runway. The smell of the kerosene at the airport did not attract me but it made sense to be close to airlines and customs; the handling of incoming airfreight was much more time-sensitive than cargo arriving by ship in Fremantle. I think I proved to be the laughingstock of every customs broker in Fremantle; they thought the centre of their existence needed to be in the port city. That made me the only freight forwarder operating an office at the airport in Perth for the next couple of years, before the competition realised the advantage we had gained and followed suit.

One of my three staff was a young Chinese lady, married to an Australian Master Mariner. David, as a ship's captain had plenty of free time whenever he had shore leave. I am still not sure what made him think about taking up flying, but I am grateful he did.

In December 1970, he and I got introduced by his wife and discovered we had the same desire to learn to fly. There was a flying club at the RAAF Base Pearce (Pearce) run by volunteers who also provided *ab initio* training for civilians like David and me. It turned to be a slightly different flying club from what I had in mind; it was a gliding operation only. The Base provided and still is a training base for future air force pilots. As a sideline, they started this gliding club to offer young cadets an alternative flying experience, since only a few actually trained to become pilots. More staff got employed on the base to provide maintenance, air traffic control and administration. The only problem seemed to be that staff rotation made it difficult to guarantee the continuous operation of the club. Because of that reason we civilians got permission to join, as we did not have to move every few months to another location.

It was all exhilarating. The base shut down for the weekend, and we were the only creatures braving the scorching sun on the field. We had the long main runway, cut by a shorter cross runway, all to ourselves; except for the millions of flies.

A small, experienced crew gave us some basic guidelines of what not to do and where to help. And help was needed; the two sail-planes on the base did not take off by themselves. First, a self-made and very simple winch needed to be positioned about 1,500 feet down the runway and a crude 10-gauge fence wire laid out on the ground, all the way to the take-off point. Just before the end of the wire, a tiny parachute was attached; its purpose eluded me until much later. Next, a basic glider was pushed into position and the rings in front of the parachute fitted into the release mechanism of the glider. This very flimsy looking contraption turned out to be our first training glider.

It was a basic design by Slingsby, in England, model T31B. The fuselage and wings comprised wooden spars covered tightly by only canvass and paint. A tandem cockpit did not have a canopy, so both pilots would stick their heads out of the plane just below the wing, which connected on top of the fuselage and secured to the fuselage on both sides with wire. The pale-looking figure in the front seat most likely belonged to a new student being trained by the instructor sitting in the back. A simple signal given by the helper holding the wing horizontal got the attention of the winch driver down the track. The engine slowly took up the slack in the wire. Full out meant the actual beginning of the launch. The winch increased speed rapidly to almost catapult the glider into the air. In less than a minute, the flying machine obtained a height of 700 to 900 feet, climbing at a steep angle. The most frightening part of the launch came at the release of the cable at the top of the launch. Imagine you are going up at a 30 degree angle when suddenly a bang and jolt underneath the glider indicates the wire has been released. At the same time, the glider's speed drops off immediately and it starts to fall out of the sky if the correct action is not taken immediately. The pilot needs to push the control stick forward, and the nose will start pointing to the ground at a shallow angle, but by this action, speed is increased again, allowing the aircraft to fly and be controlled. We had registered the theory in our brains, but the reality of the process took some time to understand through detailed training sessions on the ground.

OK, I was literally hooked; I wanted to learn how to control an aircraft and understand what makes gliders fly, even if there is no engine giving a helping hand.

After an initial introductory flight, David and I learned about the basic physics that keep an airplane in the air. The rudder, elevator and ailerons are movable parts on a plane, which help the pilot maintain control of the aircraft in flight, but there is still that vexing question of why the whole plane, including the pilot, doesn't just drop out of the sky.

To keep it simple, the explanation was that the wing of an airplane is shaped so that air moving over a wing at speed will create a vacuum, sucking the wing up, and the air flowing under the wing will assist by pushing the wing up. There is a complicated calculation to shape the wing to perform to the required specifications, but we did not bother with the detail. All we needed to understand was that the airflow over and under the wing is the key to staying in the air. Since we had no engine and propeller to assist us, we had to make sure that the glider attitude always pointed down slightly towards the earth to keep up a steady airflow over the wing. In other words, you are always falling out of the sky but in a controlled fashion.

Engines and propellers help keep the airplane up in the air but not entirely by pushing air over the wings. Instead, all the mechanical action aims to pull the aircraft forward by using the propeller, whose blades are actually tiny shaped wings. By rotating the propeller through the air at speed, it creates a forward motion of the plane. The faster the forward motion, the higher the airflow over the wing. At one point, the airflow is strong enough to create sufficient vacuum and pressure over and under the wing to get the aircraft into the air.

Simple, but the glider needs help to get airborne, and our solution was the winch system, as mentioned earlier. And that became the dilemma. We desperately wanted to fly, but if nobody wanted to drive the winch, no one would. David and I had to knuckle down and curb our impatience by learning how to handle the winch. It is not a comfortable position to sit on an old tractor seat in a wire cage to operate the powerful V8 engine driving the winch drum. To feed the wire back into the drum, a simple guiding device welded in front positioned the wire evenly on the drum.

Plenty of minor problems hampered the operation. It was not just to get the glider safely airborne by controlling the speed of the launch. Once the wire dropped, the little parachute I had described before came into its own. The parachute was supposed to slow down the drop of the wire to the ground to give the winch driver a chance to reel in the wire at high speed. No problem if the wind pointed straight down the runway, but with a crosswind, the wire moved at an angle across the field. That was not a problem, except the runway had lights positioned on each side to guide the poor jet pilot students on landing. A few times, the falling wire wrapped itself around one of those expensive runway lights, and the Base Commander appeared to be an unhappy man the next day.

To prevent that, we needed to stop the winch, let the wire drop and start walking into the field full of scratchy plants to retrieve the wire and position it again on the tarmac. I think I mentioned the millions of flies before?

I learned that fence wire gets hot when dragged out from the winch to the launching point. This is because the hard tarmac surface scrapes the thin wire, and it gets hot and soft. Whilst this makes it easier to handle the wire, it also makes it easier to break when putting on a load, such as launching a glider. If that happens, the real fun begins as a winch driver. A search has to be conducted to find both ends of the wire, detangle it and splice it again with a crude metal tool. Since this is a single strand wire, it cannot really be spliced. The only way is to use at least one foot of each end, twist them around each other using the tool and hope for the best. Finally, the real test of your splicing ability comes when the next launch occurs. The poor pilot in the glider is never sure if the wire fix will hold but has no choice and must pull back the control stick to gain height. It is disturbing when a jolt indicates that the twisted wire pulls tight. Is it going to hold, or is it going to break again?

If it breaks, the pilot is busy making decisions. Nose down immediately to maintain airflow over the wing to keep control. Check height and distances and make a safe decision to land the glider by turning around, or decide if it was prudent to land directly in front. Often, the latter proved to be the case, but since we had between 1,700 to 2,400 metres of runway in front of us we had no issue with that. You just had to make sure you missed the winch standing in the middle of the runway.

It made sense to have the winch driver sitting in a mesh cage as a wire break under pressure would create recoil that could be pretty exciting – or even dangerous – for the winch driver if they were not protected.

We earned our good deed points over time and finally got to jump into the glider, get some instructions and start the real flying lessons. I must admit that the experience of driving the winch helped me greatly to understand the safety requirements of launching and flying.

Saturday meant a day of action at RAAF Base Pearce for us poor earthlings aspiring to fly in the sky. The Airforce conducted their flying activities only during the week, and we had the airfield to ourselves. Even before my first official flight training, I had to attend to the major tasks of every operational day. Push the glider out to the launching point, inspect the flying machine to ensure that all bolts and nuts are tight and secure, and check the controls to satisfy the pilot that everything is functioning correctly. Then the rostered crew for the winch operation got busy laying out the launch cable and positioning the winch down the runway, ready for action.

A quick briefing by the instructor updated us on the wind and weather. As the first pilot in training, I positioned myself in the front seat of the Slingsby T31B glider. It is exhilarating to sit in the cramped position of the cockpit underneath the wing, looking out at the surroundings. The various instruments on the panel in front provide information during the flight on the speed, height above the ground and a clever device showing the ascent rate. In addition, I saw a small air bubble in a glass tube which looked like a builder's level on a construction site. My immediate thought was that it would show me how to evenly level my wings during the flight, but it proved to be more sophisticated. The device showed how the pilot performed to maximise the use of the rudder and ailerons. Something which I did not understand until many lessons later.

After securing my seatbelt, the instructor took his place behind me. I hoped he had a clear view towards the front because I partially blocked his view. The tow cable was attached just under the nose of the glider, and a fellow student lifted the wing so that we faced the runway in a level position and then waved his arms slowly. It confused me at first because the number of flies on this hot summer morning required a frantic action to keep them out of your face. The arm signal indicated to the winch driver to take up the slack in the cable. At that moment, the fellow on the wing tip waved his arms quickly, and the cable pulled the glider forward at a rapid pace. Before I knew it, we catapulted into the air at an angle of about 30 degrees and a speed of 50 to 60 knots. From my experience as the winch driver, I knew this would not last long as the cable would soon be dropped to earth when the glider reached a reasonable height. Even though I knew what would happen, the action of suddenly losing speed and pushing the nose of the glider downwards brought butterflies to my stomach, reminiscent of a wild ride at the showground in my childhood.

This manoeuvre created sufficient airflow over the wings to keep the glider flying without being pulled by the cable. Physics dictated that there is only one way to go, and that is down. It is only a question of how quickly we would meet the ground again, which depended on the final height we achieved with the launch. Luckily, we gained around 700 feet, which gave us a reasonable chance to turn the glider around and perform a circuit as prescribed by the manual. I had little to do with all that. My stomach decided to be in upheaval, my brain being pushed to absorb all the details and I would not have been able to make a sensible decision. That is why you have an instructor in charge; they may just save your life.

The entire flight lasted only three minutes. But, to me, it felt like a lifetime, being partially exposed to the elements in the open cockpit, being violently thrust into the sky, only to fall out after a few seconds and then taking a steep turn to fly back to land.

Slowly I made sense of all the actions. The launch height depends significantly on the pilot pulling up into the sky with reasonable force to gain height. A headwind will improve the launch. The idea is to go as high as possible to have enough time after the release to do a quick search for a source of hot air bubbles, which help to keep a glider in the air or even gain height. An almost impossible mission, as the limitations of the winch launch and the type of glider we trained in gave us little chance to do more than a quick turnaround. One of the primary measures of glider performance is the ability to keep floating in the air as far as possible, which is expressed in a measure called glide ratio. If a modern glider has a glide ratio of 50:1, it translates into the theoretical fact that this glider could fly for 50 km over the ground if starting at 1 km of height. The average performance glider has a ratio of 30:1 to 40:1.

In comparison, our Slingsby T31B glider had a glide ratio of 17:1; we admired this craft as a flying brick. Mind you, a Boeing 707 jet has the same glide ratio, as I was later told by an airline captain. However, they rarely test this ability unless their engines stop.

Our training continued, and as I got more confidence in the glider and myself, the great day finally arrived. Finally, the instructor took pity on my desperation and told me to go up my own on the next flight.

As you can see, I am still around to tell the tale. Yes, I was apprehensive, but after 55 training flights with an instructor, I must have learned enough to conduct this flight with no problems. At least, that's what I told myself repeatedly. With a cool manner, I climbed into the cockpit, secured the harness and started my cockpit checks. This time it required not just rattling off the right words to keep the instructor happy, but I needed to understand each vital step for a safe flight operation.

The ground crew was ready, the launch cable got hooked to the glider after another safety check by performing a cable release on the ground. Satisfied that all mechanical details were covered, I had to get my head organised to concentrate on the launch and be prepared for action. It must have been only seconds, but many thoughts crowded my brain, and it felt like hours. What could go wrong? Would I get sufficient height on the launch to be able to safely turn and land back at the launching point? To ensure that, I would need to really pull back on the 'joystick' during the quick launch to gain the height required. A panicked thought entered: what would happen if the cable broke again? Did I remember the correct procedure? Of course, I did, but decisions have to be made fast to avoid accidents when things happen. Whatever happens, the pilot must be ready to respond.

Pushing these thoughts away, I signalled the guy on the wing, and he waved his arms slowly, and the cable pulled taut. The next phase was a blur. I remember the glider being pulled forward, the tail banging the ground before I gained sufficient speed to get airborne. Pulling back the control stick as far as I dared, I felt the strain on the cable when some old knots started to pull together. That is an uncomfortable sensation as it might mean the cable could break at any second. I reduced the pressure by easing the ascent slightly, knowing that I would sacrifice height above the ground for a safe return flight to the starting point. The choice was made, and a few anxious moments later, we reached the top of the launch. No more height to be gained, and I had to release the cable. A weightless feeling in my stomach told me I was about to fall out of the sky. The training kicked in, and I pushed the control stick forward to get the nose down and gain speed. Next, I had to check my position, height and wind to make a fast decision to turn around to fly back or land straight ahead on the runway for safety reasons. By then, I had perspired a lot, since my instructor was on the ground, and I had to make all the decisions. I was confident that I could make it back to the launch point and made a steep turn to join the circuit, as the training prescribed.

Something went wrong. The ground came up faster than I anticipated, which meant not enough height to complete the circuit safely. Another panic, but during the training, we had been practicing for just such an event. To land the glider halfway up the runway, it required a steep turn rather than risking getting back to the launching point. Later I learned what it meant to shorten the circuit.

It took the crew some time to get to me to push the glider back a long way to the launching point. That gave me a little time to relax before I had to confront the instructor for the debriefing, which I did not look forward to. Although confident I made all the right decisions, you never know what an experienced pilot would think. We discussed the flight at length, and concluded that I may have reacted over cautiously when the cable knots tightened out of fear of a cable break. However, there was nothing wrong with the decision to make an early turn to land midway on the runway. An attempt to complete the circuit may have ended up in an accident. Relieved but mentally and physically exhausted, I decided to have a rest for the day.

The question that entered my mind was: what is this flying in a glider all about? It certainly was not the ability to stay aloft for flights lasting 4 to 6 minutes, which does not allow for fancy manoeuvres. Two flights with an instructor showed me that longer flights can be achieved by using warm air pockets rising from the ground. If the warm air rises faster than a glider flies down and the pilot manages to enter the rising air pocket, he can actually gain a higher altitude. One demonstration I experienced was in an exciting flight in the hot smoke from a ground fire lit by a farmer in his paddock. We got up a couple of 100 metres, came out of the smoke coughing and got pulled down again by the cold air feeding the fire on the ground. Back into the smoke to gain more height; we continued to work on that several times. I really worried the canvas wings on the glider would catch fire from embers, but we made it and got a little record of 50 minutes of flying time in this primary glider.

After many solo flights in the T 31B, it was time to look for a more sophisticated machine to fly; I really wanted to hone my skills to stay up in the air for longer flights by using rising warm air pockets, which we called thermals. The thought of doing that without getting smoke into my lungs certainly gave me an incentive to investigate the options of other gliding clubs. Unfortunately, RAAF Base Pearce did not provide more advanced training because of the limited operation and restricted military airspace.

Members talked about a Gliding Club in Narrogin (NGC). In operation for only about five years, it had provided training to many aspiring pilots. The fleet of gliders they operated became a great incentive for several of us to contemplate a move away from Pearce to gain more flying experience.

One of my instructors at Pearce, Dennis McNeal, tried his best to convince me that there was a lot more to learn at the Base and invited me for a demonstration flight in the other available glider, called a Kookaburra. Designed and manufactured in Australia by Edmund Schneider in Adelaide, the ugly-looking, bubbly-nosed glider had been built with wooden spars and stretched canvas over the wings to create a sturdy airplane capable of taking a lot of stress without breaking apart. The two-seat cockpit seemed to be a strange arrangement as the pilot would sit on the left, and the passenger or student would sit beside him but slightly in the back.

It looked all lopsided, but this craft's flying capability exceeded those of our trusty training glider, the Slingsby T31B.

The winch launch for the demonstration flight gained us over 900 feet in height. Dennis caught a small thermal, and we slowly climbed to about 3,000 feet above the ground. I was amazed at what could be done by simply having a better performing aircraft and did not realise that the pilot's skill made all the difference. Now that we had gained the height, Dennis would not waste it. Since we were not able fly far in any direction because of the restricted airspace around the base, he demonstrated what else could be done with an aircraft. He did warn me, but I was macho enough to agree as I wanted to see what he tried to show me.

The glider suddenly dived towards the earth, increasing speed up to 115 knots. Dennis gently pulled the control stick back until the nose of the glider rose into the sky but kept on turning until the earth came into sight again. A loop in a glider? I would not have believed it. My stomach behaved just OK as the pressure of coming out of the dive created a body that seemed to be double the weight as if standing safely on the ground. That is called a G-force. G stands for gravity on the ground, to which the body is subjected under normal conditions.

OK, I understood the concept, but my stomach was not quite at ease yet. What happened next was unexpected and created reactions and emotions which I did not know I possessed. After coming out of the loop, Dennis increased the speed again, pushing the nose almost vertically to the ground until pulling up, creating a G force of at least 2.5. My eyes bulged, cheeks dragged down my face, and my body pressed very hard onto the seat. There was something different in the flight pattern as we did not complete the loop but seemed to head straight to the sky. That reduced the speed rapidly, reducing the airflow over the wings, which also meant almost no directional control. After the intensive noise created by the wind rush on the dive, the quietness on top of the ascent became eerie, not to speak of the experience of a lightweight body. Then, again, physics took over. The momentum going up stopped and, having no way to control the aircraft's direction, there was only one way to go. Down. Sliding down tail first. There is no way to fly an aircraft backwards, and something had to happen. Would the tail break off, resulting in a horrible crash? Dennis seemed to be very calm and just waited until the weight of us in the cockpit turned the aircraft around to again face the earth. The airflow over the wings increased to give the pilot control of movement, and he gently came out of the dive to start the circuit for a perfect landing. He told me he had just performed an aerobatic manoeuvre called a 'hammerhead', but emphasised that I should never attempt it because most aircraft could not withstand the positive and negative forces created by such an action.

Well, I was very impressed with all that. However, there remained the fact that longer thermal flights and flying across the country would not be possible out of RAAF Base Pearce with its limited airspace. So I needed to join up somewhere else. Dennis understood my reasoning; he also had greater ambitions to become a jet fighter pilot. As it turned out, he topped his flying school, flew the latest jet fighters the Australian Airforce offered and became a respected aerobatic performer in different aircraft at many air shows around the country.

Narrogin airfield is about 10 km west of the town. During WWII, it was developed for the RAAF to provide an alternative airfield in case of an invasion of main Australian cities by the Japanese. That required that at least one runway would have sufficient length and width to accommodate larger aircraft. Both sides were lined with simple kerosene runway lights, which had to be lit manually in case of need, to enable planes to land at night. A second emergency runway in a north/south direction allowed for changing wind conditions.

Later, a group of farmers and residents formed the Narrogin Gliding Club (NGC) on the same airfield and started a successful training programme. After a few years, the club looked to attract new members to expand the operation.

The chief attraction for me was the chance to fly their single-seater Skylark. The members welcomed any newcomer with open arms, explained their operation and briefed visitors on what needed to be done to join their club. After a full tour of the facilities, I had to learn how to fly this glider. Part of this process involved having two check flights with an NGC instructor to show my flying skill level and familiarise me with the local circuit procedure. These checks had to done in another two-seater glider called Blanik. Mainly built from aluminium, it was considered a safe and advanced performance trainer.

Finally, I got into the cockpit of the Skylark. Although still crafted with wooden spars and canvas-covered wings, it had gained an excellent reputation for its performance and pleasant flying characteristics. The final briefing consisted of the pre-take-off checks, and finally, the ground crew hooked me to the tow rope, ready for the launch.

I had to admit, I was very excited. I had had many solo flights before, but this time it would be in a single-seat glider with a much better performance ratio than anything else I had experienced before. The first two flights needed just standard circuits to get used to the controls and landing procedure. No attempts to thermal to extend the flying time; I just wanted to get a feel for how the glider controls responded and how to conduct a safe flight. Therefore, the flying times clocked only 14 and 12 minutes, respectively. But what an improvement to my previous flights at Pearce, which lasted only 3 to 6 minutes.

When I launched my third flight in the Skylark, I decided to explore what I could do with my newly gained skills. Wow, I clocked 43 minutes on that flight, followed by another one with only 13 minutes.

Clearly I was hooked and immediately signed up to become a member of Narrogin Gliding Club.

Only two weeks later I visited NGC again, looking forward to having another enjoyable experience flying the Skylark.

Well, I admired the beautiful, handcrafted wooden spars of the tail and parts of the wing. Unfortunately, the rest of the glider had to be put to rest forever after an accident which destroyed this fine machine. I was told that a pilot with a Private Pilot's Licence (PPL) got permission to fly in this glider and crashed it due to a low circuit which prevented him from making it back to land safely. Power pilots forget that there is no recovery from a low-level flight if you do not have an engine to pull you up again. This pilot paid dearly for that mistake. He crushed both legs, underwent surgery, and went through a prolonged recovery after that event.

There was another attractive operation in place at NGC.

At Pearce, we had to launch every flight with a winch and wire or use an old V8 car to pull the wire and glider into the air. That was very cumbersome and time-consuming. In NGC, we used a little power airplane to tow gliders into the air. Yellow Bird was an old Auster airplane that had almost been dunked into yellow paint, making it highly visible. Somewhat outdated, it did not have an electric starter. One person had to swing the propeller until the engine started firing up. That turned out to be an exciting operation. The pilot would sit in the cockpit and lock the wheel brakes. He then had to open the fuel valve. The outside helper turned the propeller anti-clockwise three times to suck in some fuel into the combustion chamber. Having completed that, the pilot would yell out that he had turned on the two magnetos to provide the required electrical circuit to start the engine. The person swinging the propeller would have to pull hard on the propeller clockwise to overcome the engine's compression until it roared into action. That was the most dangerous time of the entire operation. When the engine ran, the propeller also turned because it had no gearing or clutch to prevent that. Whoever spun the propeller had to be positioned so that a forward surge of the aircraft would not put him in contact with the propeller. Even when the pilot locked the brakes, many accidents happened, with an unfavourable outcome for the poor guy spinning the propeller.

The launch procedure became a familiar process.

When the Auster made the right noises, the power aircraft would be positioned about 180 feet in front of the ready to launch glider and hook on the tow rope as we used to do with a winch launch. Then, with arm gestures, the signal had to be given to the tow pilot to take up the slack in the rope and start the launch. First, a gentle movement, and no catapult action of a winch launch. Once both airplanes gained speed, they flew, and the tow would typically take the glider up to a height of around 2,000 feet. Then the glider pilot would release the tow rope by pulling a handle inside the cockpit. Both airplanes would turn to avoid each other's flight path, e.g. a right turn for the glider and a left turn for the power plane. It was up to the skills of the glider pilot to find a thermal to extend the flight, gain height or even fly over the country for many kilometres if the conditions proved favourable.

All that excitement proved enough for me to look forward to learning more about flying in NGC, even if my original dream of using the Skylark had literally been shattered.

The decision became easy; I wanted to do more in gliding than spend time driving the winch to launch gliders or fly an outdated sail-plane for short circuits at RAAF Base Pearce.

Since the Skylark had become history, I looked for further training in the Blanik L 13 glider, which represented the pride and joy of NGC. The two-seater all-metal glider became an ideal training aircraft, allowing instructors to demonstrate all phases of flying safely. That included aerobatics. The cockpit shape reminded me of a bathtub, and climbing in and out proved to be a similar experience. Sit on the side, place each hand on either side and slowly lower yourself into the comfortable well. Sitting quite deep, it also gave a feeling of safety, as if the thin metal skin would protect you from any danger you might encounter.

My hope to fly this better-performing glider was dampened as I only got into the seat when being checked out for approval to fly another single-seater. Since the Blanik had a glide ratio of 27:1, it was considered a hot machine compared to my first training aircraft, the Slingsby T31B, with a taunting a glide ratio of only 17:1.

My dream of flying solo in a single-seater again came true when I got permission to fly the Grunau Baby II for the first time. This glider was another creation of Edmund Schneider in Adelaide, who also built the Kookaburra. A light construction, with a tiny cockpit and no fancy instruments; it looked inviting to be taken for a flight. To sit in the cockpit was different; I felt so much more exposed to the world around me without the solid metal cockpit of the Blanik. A light wind and small thermal activity made this first flight a pleasure. The controls were very responsive because the glider was so light that even a weak thermal could be centred easily, quickly going up. And why did I only manage 9 minutes on the first two flights? Call it inexperience and the need to feel comfortable performing a safe circuit and landing with an unfamiliar glider. On my next few flights, I improved my record by increasingly being more confident and managed flights which extended from 25 minutes to two hours. My exhilaration completely blocked out the physical discomfort of sitting in a cramped position for such a long period.

It took some time for me to realise that this little machine presented a few problems when flying in not so calm conditions. Climbing in thermals proved easy, but it got a bit rough in strong summer air activities, when thermal strength jumped from 4 to 9 metres per second. That is like using a lift with sudden speed changes when going up or down. OK, fear can be overcome by tightening the seat belts, making you part of the glider. I tried that later on commercial flights in rough weather, and it always worked. The other issue was the light weight and the shape of the glider. I later learned what it meant; this flying machine had no penetration into the wind. I found this out by trying to compete in a small cross country competition. The experienced pilots got the better gliders; I had to make do with the Grunau Baby. Several gliders took off on the task, only about 100 km heading east and returning via Cuballing, a little town about 10 km from Narrogin Airfield.

I bravely followed as I gained good height over the airfield. The idea was to head east, but I actually travelled backwards. There was a strong headwind blowing, and that is where the penetration bit comes into it. The wind blew me back, and to prevent that, I had to put the nose down to gain speed which gave me a chance to gain some distance into the task. The problem with that tactic is that the glide ratio is being drastically reduced with higher airspeed. As a result the ground became very close on many occasions, forcing me to find a thermal again to gain height. It's no problem to achieve that, but it is like treading water in a flowing river; you get pushed downhill. I was forced back to the Narrogin Airfield, arriving at a high altitude, but had to head east again to get back on to the task. I played this game for nearly three hours, and I think I made it as far as Cuballing only once. When all other competitors returned in their flying machines, I gave up. I landed having completed a flight time matching the other competitors but going nowhere. There was only one way to describe my mood; frustration.

Since this creation of Mr Schneider did not impress me, I was not sure what to think about my next experience with one of his machines. However, NGC had acquired two gliders, both manufactured by Schneider. The KA 6, a two-seater and the Boomerang as a single-seater claimed to have a glide ratio of around 32:1, quite impressive considering the Grunau Baby did not exceed 17:1.

I got converted into the Boomerang, and my first flight lasted exactly eight minutes. Not because of my incompetence; I was grateful to get the conversion flight and I promised to be back on the ground quickly to allow some hotshot pilot to take this glider on a cross-country run. Meanwhile, I had to get my backside into the KA 6 whenever it was not needed for training flights. Heavier than the Boomerang, it had good penetration, with an equal glide ratio. I impressed myself when I had my first solo flight, lasting three hours and 35 minutes. I improved that performance by flying for 5½ hours the next day. The world of gliding really opened up for me at this stage.

To get a booking for a glider proved to be difficult and for that reason I took any glider available just to fly. I switched from KA 6 to the Boomerang; occasionally, I got hold of the Blanik and finally got approval to carry passengers. It is easy to forget the responsibility attached to that promotion, when you can introduce a mere pedestrian to the art of flying and impress that poor person with your flying skills. Actually, I found out that I also learned a lot on these flights. Some intelligent passengers dared to ask questions, and I had to catch up quickly with my knowledge to make sure I was up to date. Naturally, I did not tell this to my flying guests as it would have ruined my self-perceived image of a totally competent pilot.

The ambition of every glider pilot is to fly long distances across the country, but that is always a challenge as weather can change quickly. Can the flight continue as planned, or should a deviation be made to look for better conditions to stay up in the air? That could also mean contemplating an unscheduled forced landing along the route if the pilot cannot find suitable uplift to stay airborne.

Part of my training required check rides with an instructor who would order me to look for a suitable place to land to get experience making safe decisions. Whenever flying at around 2,000 feet, it is recommended to look for a paddock and plan a controlled landing. I am not good at judging and inspecting a paddock looking so small from that height. The farming country is not exactly parkland, and there are many obstacles to look for. Apart from the length to allow a safe landing, I had to look for livestock roaming around the field, power lines or fences crossing the intended landing strip and heaps of rocks that the farmers built whenever they cleaned up their property. With more experience, I also saw depressions in the ground formed by livestock trampling along the same path repeatedly. Those ruts are harsh on the landing wheel and should be avoided.

Meanwhile, I had to find another thermal to avoid all the drama of landing, but I kept an eye on the altimeter to make sure I had sufficient air under the wings to conduct a safe circuit. That also meant I had to judge the wind strength and direction, as it is always preferred to land straight into the wind to maintain airspeed and keep control of the glider while reducing ground speed. It is highly recommended to aim for a short rollout on a landing in paddocks just in case an obstacle has not been detected.

I was glad I had received this training, which saved my neck on several occasions.

With the weather improving towards summer, NGC conducted a gliding competition, inviting other WA clubs to participate. I was keen to join, but still being considered a rookie, I did not have a great choice on the type of glider to use. I ended up with the Boomerang, not my favourite machine.

My five flying days during the competition were packed with action. I spent 16 hours in the air, but I also clocked up five out-landings. On my first day in the competition, I thought I was getting the hang of it all, but that proved to be a premature emotion. After 200 minutes of struggling with the elements, I conceded I could not make it back to the airfield. In lay terms, it translated that I ran out of air. There was no panic, but disappointment that I was obviously not good enough to complete the task. Choosing a paddock represented no problem with plenty of space below me, not a single moving head in sight and fences far apart. I felt proud about my choice, and the subsequent landing turned out to be near perfect. Then it dawned on me that I was far away from any civilisation and had to find help. After securing the glider with one wing pegged to the ground, I started walking towards a range of hills. Most farmers build their homes high on the grounds and logic compelled me to look there for help.

We are talking about the year 1972. There were no mobile phones to alert somebody, no GPS to guide you to the nearest dwelling. There is always hope to find a farmhouse with a telephone to alert my ground crew back at Narrogin Airfield to come and pick me up. When I finally found a house, it appeared to be deserted. At that time, many farmers had called it quits; the hard work and drought and the ever-extending bank mortgages made it just too hard to continue. Bad for them, bad for me. I spotted an old power line and followed it across several fields before my luck finally kicked in. An occupied farmhouse with friendly people concerned about where I had come from. I tried to show them on my map where I had landed and was shocked when they told me that little spot on my map was at least 30 km away. That seemed impossible as I had only walked for about 50 minutes to get this far; something had gone seriously wrong. The friendly country people guided me to their telephone, and I contacted my crew and gave them the farm's address to pick me up first.

Several cups of tea and long discussions made it a pleasant interlude and kept the nagging thoughts out of my head.

The crew arrived, we located my glider, and after disassembling the wings, we loaded it on a trailer. There is not much I remember of our discussions on the way back. I just scratched my head and wondered how I had ended up some 30 km away from the point I had marked on the map. Navigation in a glider had to be done by using a simple compass, a map on your knees to check locations below you and a healthy amount of optimism that you did it all correctly. Again, no GPS, no radio, just the sun parching you under the plastic canopy of the glider; no wonder that rational thinking became difficult.

Totally embarrassed when returning to NGC I had to relate my story. Cross-checking the location of the farmer's place, we established that I actually ended up 30 degrees off my planned course. Yes, they called me a rookie at this game, but surely I could not be that ignorant?

One of my earlier instructors from Pearce had become an instrument fitter by profession and experienced in evaluating rookies' performances. Just as well, John had some faith in me and suggested to 'swing the compass' of my glider. The compass was still fixed in the glider's cockpit, and to my amazement, we positioned the glider on a marked grid facing north. We then moved the glider facing east, south and west. At each position, we checked the compass and measured. The final result confirmed that the magnetic fields of the compass did not show the correct directions, which explained why I was 30 degrees off my course. Repairs got initiated. Meanwhile, I began feeling a little less like an idiot but bemoaned the fact that I should have picked up the differences between the landmarks below and my map to recognise that I was headed in the wrong direction.

There is always another day to improve, and I prepared myself for another day of the contest with more confidence.

The next day, the task in the competition proposed a flight to Kulin and back. My confidence was high, the weather forecast promising, and I took off to battle with the more experienced pilots in the field. It is exhilarating to monitor a bunch of gliders circling in the same thermal to gain height. It also increased my blood pressure when I meekly joined the same gaggle of gliders competing to centre their craft in the thermal to gain maximum lift. I constantly turned my head watching out for the other planes turning around, so I lost orientation and ended up at the far side of the rising warm air and gained little height.

On the other hand, it gave me an advantage to be far below the rest of the gang with plenty of space to manoeuvre. There are safety rules when joining and flying in the same thermal. A vertical separation of 200 feet may be comfortable for an experienced pilot, but for a rookie like me, it was more of an enforced nightmare. Wow, what a relief when the lot suddenly decided they had enough height gain and took off to continue the task; I was left alone to make decisions without pressure.

I experienced the same scenario again during the first hour but then lost track of the competitors because they flew far in front of me. Now, I actually began to enjoy myself, staying up and following in the right direction on the task since my compass had been repaired. I had time to compare my map with what I recognised on the ground. Finally, Kulin came into sight. Competition rules required us to fly around the wheat silo and take a picture over the wing as proof that we had made it so far. That silo seemed in sight for a very long time. It felt as if I would never get there, but persistence and some heavy breathing exercises got my nerves under control, and I turned at the correct time, took my picture and went back on my homeward track. That day, I actually made it back to the Narrogin airfield without having to land in some scrubby paddock. I was very proud of myself; after all, I had completed the task, although it took me five hours and 25 minutes to complete the 200 km distance.

On arrival, the airfield appeared to be too quiet, with no activity to be seen until I got back to the club house. All the competitors were assembled there, relaying their hero stories of how they flew that day and having a few drinks. Most of them got back within three hours as the thermals had been excellent, and it was only me who struggled to stay aloft. I did not care. I managed to come back. I had great fun after overcoming some worrying experiences. I learned a lot by simply comparing my actions with those of the other competitors. Obviously, I still had to learn a lot about the theory and praxis of flying across the country. A degree in weather forecasting might have helped.

The next few days were not so successful. Flying a short task because of stronger wind conditions, I had to decide to land just a few kilometres away from the airfield. I might have made it back, but caution is better than a gamble.

And another day of failure followed. A great flight of over four hours got me back a bit late in the afternoon, when it cooled down, and it became difficult to find thermals to keep me up. I did not want to make the same mistake as on my first day when I landed in a paddock without checking for the next inhabited dwelling to ask for help. This time I made an early decision as the small field next to the country town of Popanyinning looked inviting. No livestock in the paddock, the fences far apart, but a power-line ran through the property in the town's direction. Luckily the line followed the street, and I could see enough space between the line and road fence to put my glider down safely.

The usual routine followed. Secure the wing on the ground and start walking into town to find a telephone to call my ground crew to pick me up. My gloomy mood picked up considerably when I found a small hotel on the main street. That meant a telephone had to be available, and I could relax with a little drink since I would not fly or drive again that day. I used the excuse that nerves do need to be calmed down.

The helpful publican nearly called the lunatic asylum when I asked if he had any fresh milk. When he confirmed that with a strange look in his eyes, I think I nearly topped him when I requested a shot of whisky to be put into the glass of milk. As a publican he obliged, keeping his distance just in case I started to grow fangs.

I finally explained to him my strange behaviour.

At the gliding club, we had quite a few drinks in the evenings. After all, the heat of 35C plus could be oppressive, and we had to get some liquid into our bodies. Unfortunately, some more sophisticated fellows introduced wine to these sessions, trying to impress everybody. The wines came in small cartons holding a plastic bag containing two litres. A convenient little tap allowed us to fill up our glasses and feel on top of the world. The quality of those wines was questionable. Soon we called the white variety Chateau Cartonnage, whereas the red wine would be classified as Chateau Chunder.

I soon found out that my stomach acted strangely after those sessions, with my head in a sorry state the following day. Not a good idea to jump into a glider under those conditions. Since I always liked milk to settle my stomach, I experimented by adding a little whisky, and it turned out perfectly. Happy at night, fresh in the morning, ready to fight another day.

I am not sure if I convinced the publican with that logical explanation, but we parted as friends when my crew finally picked me up.

One little episode might be of interest. But I warn you if you have a weak stomach turn the page quickly.

Gliding relies mainly on warm air rising into the sky. That means long hours in a small cockpit with a plastic glass bubble over your head, which dehydrates you like a fish in the sun. To prevent loss of concentration for lack of fluids in the body, you need to hydrate by drinking whatever is non-alcoholic to keep you going. The problem is to know how much you need or how much is too much.

One competitor found out the hard way. Being a hotshot pilot, he went on a long task taking a few hours. He diligently drank his water, and everything was fine. Until he had problems with his bladder building up pressure, about to burst. It did not need a complicated calculation to realise that he would never make it back to the airfield on time. A decision had to be made. All planes usually carry a small package to assist those poor souls who experience airsickness and need to fill a bag. Our poor pilot felt blessed and used this bag to relieve his pain.

When flying, you are somewhat busy with both hands and legs to keep the aircraft under control; it is not advisable to hold a bag in your hand. The pilot, therefore, placed it carefully on the floor of the cockpit and carried on with his fantastic flight. He returned to the airfield at a perfect time after completing the task. He experienced elation about his possible win of the day that he thought he had to celebrate with a loop over the field. Everybody on the ground was impressed, but the pilot made one minor mistake. If you make a loop, it is normal that the speed on top of the loop is much reduced before you start your rapid descent towards the earth, completing the recovery phase. Our poor chap did not cater for that, and the bag so carefully placed on the cockpit floor did what is expected to do in such circumstances. The centrifugal force of a rotating aircraft was replaced by earth gravity. The bag fell on the poor chap. After landing, nobody wanted to help him out of the glider.

After our friend cleaned out his glider and had an extensive hot shower, he joined us for a heavy night of drinking to recover from his unfortunate mishap.

Cunderdin Airport has been and still is the base of the Gliding Club of Western Australia. That makes the club the second oldest in Australia since formation at Caversham Airfield in 1944.

The move to Cunderdin airfield provided the club with ready-made facilities, including sealed cross runways and established buildings which now function as the operation/social centre of the club.

During WWII, Cunderdin was used for training Air Force pilots, using mainly the now quaint looking Tiger Moth dual-wing airplane. During that time, the airfield was upgraded to suit pilot training. The gliding club took full advantage of the established infrastructure.

My further training took place at Cunderdin. Highly qualified instructors put a few pilots through a demanding program to learn about the theory and practice of safe flying. After five days, I was pleased to be considered good enough to be elevated to the status of an Assistant Flying Instructor.

I did not know it but we poor chaps glowing with pride on our promotion were destined to be used as the basic training slaves for new pilots. We had qualified to put a newcomer through the *ab initio* training, followed by coaching on soaring and cross-country flying. The only restriction was that we could not send a newly qualified person solo; that means to let him loose in the sky on his own. That privilege still belonged to the Full Instructor, but with that authority came the responsibility to assess the new pilot as being fully qualified to conduct his first solo flight and land safely.

My gliding activity became busy after that. I may not be a hotshot cross country pilot, but I tended to be in big demand to train new enthusiasts to learn to fly. Fledgling gliding clubs started up in Byford and Beverley and, always short of instructors, they needed help. It was great because I could show off my relatively new skills and fly without incurring a cost myself.

That rosy picture turned a bit dark after flying at Byford a few times. The club was just outside the township, using a reasonably sized paddock as a landing strip. The weather was almost predictable to the hour. Located not so far from the coast, we could almost set our watch on when the so-called Fremantle Doctor would arrive. The sea breeze brought cool air, thermal activities stopped, and flights became short. Launch, circuit, landing. Suitable for training new guys, but there was a slight problem. Because of the prevailing wind, the direction of landing on the strip gave only one option. That meant planning the circuit carefully as the beginning of the strip began close to the road. Along the road were high voltage power-lines, which meant a high approach was needed with a sharp descent after the power-lines had been cleared. No problem for experienced pilots, but students did not feel comfortable in that situation and started to quit. The club did not survive for long, and I admit I was somewhat relieved because the safety aspect of the entire operation appeared marginal.

The Narrogin Gliding Club decided to organise a gliding expedition to the Stirling Ranges. Many theories around the existence of wave conditions in that area had been discussed. A wave is a constant wind reflected by a hill or mountain range, and a glider can ride the top of this wave. If the wind is strong, a second and third wave can occur behind the mountain range. These waves can go up to great heights, not accessible by riding a thermal in normal conditions. The goal was to explore the conditions in the Stirling Ranges and try to set new records of height gains up to 25,000 feet.

Studies showed that the strongest winds would happen in the wintertime. Steady northerly winds deflected on the steep cliffs of Bluff Knoll; the wave would then go up and get pressed down on the back of the mountain only to come up again in a second, much stronger wave in greater heights.

September looked to be the best time. Early scouting had indicated a suitable paddock near to the entrance to the National Park; the farmer who owned this property allowed us to use this field. We could set up camp in the little forest next to the paddock.

The caravan of cars, equipment and fuel went by road. One plane launched in Narrogin and towed a glider behind to arrive at the paddock about 90 minutes later. All arrived safely, but the landing on the proposed strip was rough. The field used to be a little forest of Mallee trees which had been cleared by the farmer to graze his sheep on the paddock. Unfortunately, all the roots of the trees had to be cleared from the ground before a regular flying operation could begin.

It must have taken a full day with everybody working hard to pile up these roots in big lots before we could start flying.

A couple of flights were conducted to test the conditions on the top of Bluff Knoll. The results were encouraging, but it seemed the wind was not strong enough yet to create the weather pattern we were looking for.

Meanwhile, we had to survive the harsh winter temperatures and some light rains. After all, this was the end of winter. We experienced very cold nights with temperatures around zero C. Tents do not keep you very warm; sleeping bags, layers of clothing and socks were needed to keep us alive. The roots we collected in great pain now became a lifesaver. Big heaps were lit up, and the hardwood burned slowly with intensive heat spreading sufficiently to anybody huddling around.

After a couple of nights in those conditions, some of the weaker species of our group decided to accept the farmer's offer of a hot shower in his house. Everybody else continued to suffer, not only from the cold but being obviously avoided by the others, who preferred to stay upwind most of the time.

This first expedition confirmed the theory that wave conditions exist in the Stirling Ranges, even though we could not achieve the height goals expected. Stronger winds from the north were required, and we could not extend our stay to wait long enough. We all decided we'd had a great time despite all the hardships. When the farmer asked us if we would return next year, we heartily confirmed our intention. He then indicated that he would be interested in starting a little camping ground. The first step was to put up a building to house toilets, showers and a common area with kitchen facilities.

Flying around Bluff Knoll was something totally new to all of us. Narrogin does not boast any large hills, and the energy source would be thermals to provide sufficient uplift for our gliders. In contrast, flying in winter conditions with no thermals was thrilling. A steady wind reflecting on the lower part of the cliff was sufficient for us to cruise back and forth in front of Bluff Knoll almost indefinitely. There were only two essential points to remember. After being dropped over the top of Bluff Knoll by the tow plane, it was time to search for the updraft in front of the mountain. The exact location would change if the wind changed slightly. Any required turn in the glider to get back into the lift had to be executed by flying away from the cliff-side. It is very hard to estimate distances to the cliff when flying below the top; any wrong turn could end up crashing into the rocks.

Bluff Knoll was about five miles away from our simple airstrip. We needed to make sure we had sufficient height at the Knoll to fly back safely to the field as in between was only dense forest and bushland. Every day, before flying begun, a safety briefing was conducted to ensure that the basic rules were embedded in our brains. The rest of the day was sheer exhilaration.

Launching the glider, having a few flights, watching the changing light reflected on the cliff and monitoring the weather kept us happily occupied. Reluctantly we finally had to pack up and return to our base in Narrogin; but we had already planned another excursion to the Stirling Ranges the following year.

I had many opportunities to convert into different gliders during 1973. That all involved another instructor assessing my abilities and having to allow me to take an unfamiliar aircraft for a solo flight.

It was all a good experience, and it helped me get a seat in a glider in Germany. I was on a short business trip which I always managed to combine with a visit to my ageing mother, who lived near Hannover. Not far away, I found a gliding club on a hillside outside a village and a busy operation, with gliders constantly towed by winch into the air. If the conditions were right, the pilot could get the ridge lift of the little hills nearby and fly back and forth, enjoying a comfortable ride, although most of the flights ended up being just a short circuit to make it back to the designated landing strip.

It seemed I did all the right things and was allowed to use a single-seater glider 'L Spatz' to have a solo flight. Being a very light aircraft, I could gain a reasonable height on the launch and happily caught a couple of thermals nearby to get me up to 1,500 feet. The altitude is measured by air pressure at sea level, but in hilly countries, allowances have to be made for elevated locations as the ground elevation might be far less than the indicated level.

There were a few hills below me but nothing to worry about; I had plenty of height to clear all those and planned an enjoyable flight in good weather.

However, nothing prepares you for the roar of jet engines and the flashing sight of two F 104 Starfighters right under your glider. Apparently, the German Airforce regularly conducted low-level training flights using ground hugging radar to hone their pilots' skills. I was not impressed but scared out of my wits; nobody had told me about this possibility before. How did I know these pilots had actually seen me and taken evasive action to avoid a collision? I had no idea what was happening, but it certainly spoiled my perfect flight. I immediately called the ground, announcing my return, and joined the circuit for landing. All was OK, but somehow my legs felt like rubber when I stepped out of the glider. The entire flight was over in just 20 minutes. It was a great shame because it was perfect weather to have a long, enjoyable flight exploring the countryside. There were just too many heavy metal pieces spoiling the air for me; I quit.

Back in Australia, I got a flight in a 'Dart 15', single-seater wooden spar glider with canvas covering the wings. It was very easy to fly and considered a well-performing glider. Experiencing the difficulties of booking a glider whenever I wanted to fly, I took the offer to join the syndicate of three guys to buy a share in this beautiful little machine. The members of the syndicate came from different walks of life. The leader was a manual arts teacher, Dennis Gorton, who had an incredible knack for fixing minor damage to the glider. Another older member was a farmer from Kulin, Alan Hockridge, and number three was an Immigration Officer, David Goodfellow. I was happy to be accepted as a new member, mainly because I was still considered a German and, therefore, a foreigner.

Summer is always busy with gliding activities. Hot weather, strong thermals and plenty of flies.

Alan, our local farmer, was happy to join the annual gliding competition in Cunderdin for a week. He had a small caravan, and we bunked in together as other accommodation was not available.

We got plenty of flights during that week, some exceeding five hours. I definitely did not win any day's competition or trophy but was a happy contributor; we supported the more hot-shot pilots who needed us to mark thermals along the route. They would expertly join our thermal, use the best part and shoot off again along the designated task, leaving us bewildered.

Another business trip coincided, purely by chance, with a visit to the local gliding club in the mining town of Mt Newman. The club was formed to provide activities for the mining community on weekends and got excellent support from a mining company. An airstrip was carved into the bush near the township. The club members had prepared an old V8 Holden utility to use as a tow vehicle to launch gliders into the air. To keep down the dust, gallons of used engine oil were poured onto the ground. Accelerating rapidly, the glider would be pulled up on the end of an 1800 feet fence wire cable to gain sufficient height to find a thermal, extending the flight. Newman was always hot and sticky; thermals were plentiful and often quite violent, making it an uncomfortable flight over the rough country around. The town was only a few kilometres away, but flying had to be restricted within gliding distance of the airstrip. If an emergency landing were required, the rocky hills extending around the town for many kilometres would prevent a safe landing even by the most experienced pilot.

The WA Gliding Association's Regional Training Office (RTO) visited this club to assess its safety standards. I'd joined that day, being mighty proud of my relatively new status of Assistant Instructor and keen to learn something new. The RTO was an air force instructor in Pearce in his real life; his name was B Goodson. Everybody called him "Bluey" because he had flaming red hair. All that was very confusing to me as 'Strine' was still not ingrained in me.

Bluey took me on a couple of flights, and I was not happy. Something inside the metal fuselage of the Blanik glider was chafing every time we used the vertical stabiliser (otherwise called the rudder).

We decided to ground the glider until we had investigated this further. Inspection holes were opened, and when we checked the control cables, we found the ones used for the rudder were loose, resulting in the scraping along the fuselage. This had to be rectified as the cable might fray and break, leading to a possible inflight disaster.

The fuselage is not exactly large, but it was possible for me to wriggle my way towards the smaller part by removing the backseat and pushing myself through the opening. I was able to tighten the cable and secure it with a cable tie. Problem solved, we went for another few flights. I gained my aerobatic certificate by demonstrating the correct executions of a loop, *chandelle*, stall turn and wingover. The *chandelle* is similar to a stall turn, except speed is maintained at all times during the exercise. These might be all very technical terms, but the action gets your adrenaline up and provides you with a very comfortable feeling once you have solid earth under your feet again.

Tony van Bergen was a technician at the RAAF Base Pearce. As members of the base gliding club, we spent many hours and days working together to launch gliders, operate the winch and get lessons from a gliding instructor on how to fly the basic contraptions, which we considered to be flying machines.

Tony was very keen to become an Air Force pilot but needed to show that he had sufficient flying experience in powered aircraft to be considered. When he joined us at the Narrogin Gliding Club, he continued to fly gliders, but the main reason was to use the power training facilities run by John Douglas, a Kiwi who lived in Narrogin and was operating the local flying school.

The number of training hours was restricted purely by the absence of sufficient funds to pay for continued lessons. It was not pure charity on my part when I suggested I would join him on some sorties and share the cost, but because I was keen to get my backside into the cockpit and gain the experience of what is possible with a powerful propeller in front of the plane.

The flying club had a small fleet of aircraft to be used by their members. Initial training would be conducted in a Cessna 150, followed by the larger Cessna 172. The real fun started when Tony got signed out to use a 'tail-dragger', a powered aircraft which had two landing wheels under the wing and one wheel or skid under the tail. The landing behaviour of such a plane was quite different and needed a lot of fine-tuning on the final approach. One of those planes was a De-Havilland DCH1 called Chipmunk, a streamlined metal plane with wings attached on the lower side of the fuselage. It was very easy to fly in calm conditions; once the trim was balanced, we could fly straight ahead without touching the controls. To come in to land meant it was back to the tricky part of touching down with the front wheels first and slowly lowering the tail onto the back wheel. Steering on the ground was only possible by having sufficient airstream generated by the propeller to make use of the rudder to turn the nose of the plane in the right direction. Too strong an airstream would increase speed and lift the tail of the ground again, not exactly what you want to do when landing.

Another fun aircraft was the DE Tiger Moth. The fuselage and double-decker wings were constructed from metal and wooden spars covered by canvas and protective paint. A tandem cockpit was open on top, one wing just above the head of the pilots. One fuel tank feeding the engine via a tube down below was in the middle of the wing. Gravity was the only power in action; there was no fuel pump or hydraulics, just operating a simple switch would let the fuel go down the line.

This plane was the early design by De-Havilland. It was used extensively for training new pilots during WWII in Australia, with a significant training centre operating at Cunderdin airfield.

The excitement of flying this plane started even before take-off. The pilot would sit in the cockpit, switch on the fuel flow and check that all his controls were fully functional. One crucial point of safety was to make sure the wheel brakes were on before the electric circuit would be switched on. At that stage, an assistant (in that case, I) had to turn the propeller slowly anticlockwise three times to suck fuel into the engine's combustion chamber. The pilot needed to open the throttle slightly. Now, the propeller had to be spun clockwise using two hands and total body weight to overcome the engine's compression. If everything was done correctly, the engine would start with a roar, the propeller would spin fast, and the poor chap in front of this spinning wheel had to step back quickly not to get his head chopped off. That's where the significance of having working brakes became very clear.

Tiger Moth and I at Jandakot Airport

After this adrenalin producing exercise, I would climb over the lower wing into the aircraft and get my straps tight and secure. Although the pilot in command would sit in the back seat, I had a better forward view directly through the propeller. The leather head covers had a tube attached through which communication was established by shouting into a small mouthpiece.

After take-off, it became a little windy in the open cockpit, but it was exhilarating to watch the earth getting a little smaller beneath the wings.

Flying straight forward becomes boring after a time; we needed action, so Tony ordered me to close my eyes so I could not see what he might do. Of course, I could sense the movement in my stomach, but when he called me to open my eyes again and take over the controls, I would find myself in an unusual situation and had to think fast about how to get back to normal, stable flight. Initially, our little game was tame, using a gentle *chandelle*, then getting more adventurous in a stall turn manoeuvre. A big thrill came from putting each other halfway into a loop before passing the controls on to see how clever the other pilot was to get out of this smoothly. It could well be that we were hanging upside down on top of the loop when the centrifugal force kept us in the seat. The ultimate test came when the loop was not executed correctly. The aircraft was flying almost horizontal upside down, and we would only be held in our seats by the seatbelt straps. If that happened a few seconds too long, the engine would not get sufficient fuel through the drip line and start to cough and finally stop working. That is not a good situation when you are sitting in an aircraft which could never be considered a glider. A typical house brick would have similar flying abilities.

Obviously, there is always an answer to the problem. A very important factor had to be considered before engaging in such activities. That was the height at which we began our game. Usually, the rules are clear; any aerobatic manoeuvre has to be conducted at a height level to complete the action and resume a normal flight with a minimum height over the ground of 1,000 feet. Well, we needed to factor that in because our recovery used up a lot of air below the wings. First, the loop had to be completed by getting up the airspeed by pointing the nose towards the ground. That would also start fuel going down the line to the engine. The propeller's spin would ignite the engine again in a similar fashion to what happens on the ground, and the pilot had control once again by using the engine power to get us back up to safer heights.

To ensure all these factors, we only conducted our little experiments when we had at least a height of 4,000 feet and plenty of airspace around us with no other traffic to be seen. Relying on hearing other aircraft would have been futile with the extreme noise level produced by our engine and the wind stream rushing past our ears.

Tony was finally accepted into the air force training at Pearce and passed his flying course with honours. His dream of becoming a fighter pilot was wiped out when he discovered a slight problem with his vision. He could fly the long-distance reconnaissance aircraft ORION for many years, but the long, boring hours spent on those missions must have finally made him decide to quit and join his family business in Melbourne.

For me, that was the signal to get my own PPL (Private Power Licence) to tow gliders into the air. I commenced my training in Narrogin and went solo after just over four hours. My gliding experience helped me understand the basic requirements to take off safely and land a powered aircraft.

The training aircraft used mainly by new students was a Cessna 150. Basically, it was a little metal box hanging on wings with a motor in front driving the propeller. The cockpit had modern instrumentation and one great little button, which was a joy to press after going through all the pre-flight checks. No more swinging the propeller; that little button was the electric starter to get the engine to turn over. There was not much space inside, and elbows could easily be used to wake up the student if he happened to fall asleep during a flight. Not that I have ever had any problem with that myself, as the inflight training was exciting enough to keep me fully awake. The experience of controlling the take-off by putting on engine power, increasing the speed and getting the airflow over the wings to give lift differed totally from a glider launch. No more outside manpower is required; you are in control of when and how you take off, as long as the engine ticks over.

Most students enjoy just flying around the countryside. To me, the take-off, performing the correct circuit and landing smoothly was the perfect challenge and gave me great pleasure when I executed it all correctly. Maybe it was the future purpose of flying in my mind, as the whole reason for me to get a PPL was to tow gliders into the air. That mainly involves a short take-off run, climbing to a pre-arranged height, and after the glider is released from the tow rope, bringing the plane back onto the landing strip as soon as possible to reduce flying time and therefore cost.

Training included several lessons on flying purely by instruments. This is a safety requirement in case a pilot is flying through clouds and cannot see where he is going. The other effect is that without seeing a horizon, humans lose orientation when flying blind. The instruments will show if the plane is flying level and straight, and the compass will indicate the plane's direction. Most accidents in cloud flying occur because the pilot could not fly level, turned and may have even ended up in a stall without knowing which way is up or down.

It is strange when the instructors put a cover on the front screen, and the only view is the instrument panel. Confidence comes with experience, and when even slight control movements are recorded by the instruments and the pilot understands the signs correctly, he can safely continue his flight by taking corrective actions if required. If not, you may read something in the paper the next day.

My power flight training continued slowly as financial restraints reduced the number of hours I could afford. Meanwhile, I kept up with my gliding in Narrogin. In addition, I helped as an Assistant Instructor at Beverley, Byford and during our annual Wave Camp at the Stirling Ranges.

Launching from the rough paddock was daunting. I could feel for the poor student sitting in front of me in the glider when we took off for the run-up to 4,200 feet at the top of Bluff Knoll at the eastern part of the Stirling Ranges. The thin tow rope connecting us to the tow plane would bend and wave whenever we hit some air turbulence until corrective action would straighten it out again with a little jolt. On coming closer to the Bluff, the tow plane in front seemed very tiny when looking at the imposing cliff of rocks. It is difficult to judge distances in the air, so we always kept away from the cliff face until we gained sufficient height to be above the top of the ridge. The tow plane would leave in a wide arc as soon as we pulled the lever to release the tow rope, and we were gliding on our own, looking for warmer air rising to keep us afloat. Warm, moist air rising can be indicated by cumulus clouds forming, but along the ridge, it will most likely be wind deflected on the slope leading up to the peak. When gaining altitude, a little instrument in the cockpit would show the speed at which the glider is going up, and the altimeter would reflect the height change.

Once confident, we would explore the ridge further to the left of Bluff Knoll, always keeping an eye on the altimeter. We did not like to be below the top of the cliff unless we knew we had no problems gaining height again. Another factor to watch was the distance to the landing strip, right behind our little forest where we used to camp. Height, distance and wind direction dictated our decisions to turn away from the Bluff and head back. It was always a good assurance to get buffeted by strong turbulence when coming over the forest as we then knew we had made it back safely to land and relax.

We had another member from the RAAF Base Pearce join us on one occasion. He acted very much like the big hot shot pilot as an Instructor at the base in Pearce.

At the Stirling Ranges, he rigged up his Blanik glider as a pretend-jet without the engine. Flying helmets for him and his passenger, fancy antennas poking out of the fuselage, impressive earphones using noise activated radio communication with his passenger. The only problem was his ego. He may have thought he could do anything in the air as if he had a powerful jet engine behind him. However, in a glider, it was not to be. When he misjudged the wind and didn't compensate with sufficient height, he made a desperate run for our landing strip until he realised he would not make it over the forest. At least he kept calm and took action not to end up crashing into the trees. He slightly diverted the plane and landed on the road leading up to the car park at the bottom of Bluff Knoll. In 1974 the road was not yet upgraded and was merely a small strip of tarmac with roadside markers too close for comfort. The plane landed OK but took out a couple of markers and damaged the wings. On the plus side there was hardly any traffic from tourists visiting Bluff Knoll, and both pilot and passenger escaped without harm; only the plane suffered considerable damage to the wings.

I had an interim job helping a friend run his business selling carpet tiles and wallpaper. One market we identified as being the mining and port towns in the Pilbara. I realised that the people up north did not really trust a company in Perth to offer shipments of goods to be delivered correctly to their doorsteps. My suggestion was to plan a trip going north and combine business with pleasure. The idea was to hire a small plane, load it up with samples of carpet tiles and wallpaper and fly up to various towns to show our wares and meet the potential buyers personally to gain their confidence.

My restricted PPL did not allow me to fly cross-country; I was not qualified. That little problem could easily be solved by inviting a young fellow from the Royal Aero Club, Perth, to be the official pilot. He needed extra hours as a commercial pilot to build up his CV. But we needed a slightly larger plane to load about 300 kilos of samples and fly long distances. We picked a Cessna 182 as suitable, but I needed some lessons first to get approval from the authorised instructor to fly this type. Finally, I was ready; we advertised our little roadshow in the local section of the *West Australian* newspaper in the towns and got good feedback from interested parties to attend a viewing. Rooms in local hotels were booked, and we were ready to fly off.

The first sector of our route would take us from Jandakot along the coast towards Geraldton, with the final destination Newman, a mining town a population of about 2,500. Most people working in town had standard company housing; it would have been difficult to distinguish one from the other, inside and outside. Money was not a big problem; they just wanted to have a little more home comforts and were prepared to pay for wall coverings and carpet tiles. That was our aim, help them out and make a bit of money in the process. Obviously, I painted a very optimistic picture in order to get the go-ahead from my friend to charter the plane and have fun flying around the countryside.

We calculated it would take five hours flying to get to Newman. I plotted the course on our navigation map and noticed a stretch of about two hours in which we only had one navigation point on the ground. Remember, there was no GPS navigation at the time; the tools were a map, a compass, the weather report and good eyesight to follow navigation points on the ground and collate those with the details on the map. That one landmark we had to spot to confirm our correct position was marked as a single farmhouse in the middle of rugged rock formations in the Pilbara. It does not bear to think about getting lost in this vast country, as any landing most likely would be a deadly crash with little chance of survival. I was young, my eyes were good, and luck had it that the roof of the old farmhouse reflected a little bright light when the angle of sunshine hit it at the right time. We got it but we were off course by about ten miles, no problem.

When getting close to Newman airport, we got reports of a fairly strong side wind. Since I had been flying all the way, I was a little tired, but crosswind did not scare me anymore as my gliding experience had taught me how to land in those conditions. When I set up the circuit and final approach, I got a few signs it was not all good. We were strongly drifting sideways and needed to compensate by steering about 20 degrees off the runway to compensate for the wind. The runway was visible through the side window instead of the front; we were coming in lower and lower, and just before hitting the tarmac, I had to push the rudder quickly into the other direction to straighten up the nose of the aircraft in line with the centre of the tarmac. That was the theory. My experience in this aircraft was limited to three landings during the conversion training in good weather conditions.

Now the wind pushed us sideways. The aircraft was much heavier because of the payload, and my speed was not perfectly coordinated to make a smooth landing. The result was not pretty. Dumping the wheels on the ground was fine as solid contact would prevent more drifting sideways. The wind pushed us in the wrong direction; I struggled to keep the wing down and pushed the rudder; it was almost a performance equalling an obstacle course. The good thing is that friction and gravity helped to control the situation. Wheels on the ground, reduced power and a bit of good luck kept us rolling in the right direction until we parked the plane in front of the little metal hut near the tarmac. I was not proud of myself but was relieved to have done my first long-distance navigation flight with little help from the official PIC (Pilot in Charge) sitting next to me.

After our long flight the day before and a well-earned rest in the motel in Newman, I got to set up my display of goods in the public area of the pub. Interest was a bit slow in the morning but picked up later on, and I made a few sales after I seemed to have gained a little trust from the wary folks in this outback town. The next day was also showing promising results, but since we had pre-booked our roadshow before, we had to pack up that night to fly to our next destination, Paraburdoo.

This even smaller mining town was only a relatively short distance away; my calculation told me it would take 30 minutes flying time. I plotted the compass track on the aviation map, and after doing my flight checks, we took off for an early morning arrival at our destination. Following the compass indications, I monitored the time as we should be able to see the little township a few minutes before arrival. The dirt airstrip was carved into the bush a few kilometres out of town; there was no air traffic control in this remote area, and the recommendation was to fly over the local pub in town first to alert somebody to come out to the airstrip to give us a lift.

That sounded all very easy, except after 28 minutes of flight time I began to fidget a little because I could not see any sign of civilization in front of us. It came up to 29 minutes, then 30 minutes, but still no sign of life below. Basic safety rules give guidelines on what to do if you get lost. The best way would be to turn around and head back to our starting point, going in the exact opposite direction following the compass. That way, we would be safe and work out what went wrong.

Well, at this stage, my young companion, who was officially in charge of flying this aircraft, pulled one of his magic tricks. Even in those days without GPS, there was a clever way of using the beams of three different radio stations to plot your position in a triangulation and make adjustments to your course if required. Luckily we flew high enough to pick up three distant radio stations and established that we were at least 20 km off course. After adjusting our heading, we finally saw the town, buzzed the pub and landed at the strip in the bush. It took a while for the transport to pick us up, but I certainly needed a break to re-think and calm down. Settling into the motel room, I pulled out my map again to recalculate and find out where I went wrong. It seemed I did everything according to the book. The compass heading, wind conditions and timing were all correct; I could not figure out why we ended up so far off course, which potentially would have been very dangerous. My trusted and more qualified pilot came to the rescue. As a fully licensed pilot, he was on the distribution list of what is called 'Notice to Airmen'. That is a newsletter with updates on changed systems or local requirements. It was there we found the notification that the town of Paraburdoo was indicated on the wrong spot on the official aviation map for that area. My calculation based on the map was correct, but the map showed the wrong location. The course I plotted was several degrees off the correct destination, which explained why we could not find the town.

Paraburdoo gave us another justification for this trip. Sales came in, and I established good communication with the townspeople, which I also adopted during Port Hedland's next and last stop. The last couple of flights were uneventful. We got back to Jandakot Airport after about 15 hours in total, flying over what could be the most uninhibited and uninviting countryside in this part of the world.

My friend/boss was pleased to see the financial results of this unusual trip and suggested planning another one soon. Although I would have loved this idea, I could not agree because the communication I set up with those towns did not warrant another expensive journey. In the future, we would just advertise in the local paper. Interested parties would cut out the little coupon and send it together with one dollar to show they were genuinely interested. Based on that, we would send small samples of wallpaper or carpet tiles, the order would come in, and we could ship it up north with no hassle. Over time I had many visitors who benefited from our system coming to our shop in Perth. They wanted to thank us for being trustworthy and diligent in following up on their orders. Happy days indeed.

My joy was a little reduced when I found out that the number of hours I flew in that aircraft would not show up in my logbook as a flight record. My pilot had a commercial licence but did not have the certificate as an instructor, which prevented me from logging the flying hours as training. Too bad, but I still got the practical experience, and the company paid for all expenses. There was really nothing to complain about.

My ambition to become a fully qualified tow pilot in the gliding club had to be put on hold at the end of 1975.

The job to help my friend in his retail business in Perth was only temporary. I finally secured a position in Taiwan starting in January 1976. More flying was involved but this time as a passenger in commercial flights, as I had to attend internal training and familiarisation in the head office of the company in Germany.

The first two years in Taipei were hectic, and there was no time to pursue my dreams of flying.

I talked to several new friends and business associates during this time, and it was suggested that we should try to start our own gliding club in Taiwan. Money to buy a glider and a winch was no obstacle; I had my

Assistant Instructors Licence and could train anybody keen on joining this little adventure.

Two main issues remained. Firstly we had to find a suitable flat piece of earth to be converted into a simple airstrip. That could be a problem as any farmland was a rough rice paddy with plenty of mud in the rainy season. Farmers were willing to sell their small properties, but the land was rare on this little island, and prices jumped up, making poor rice farmers millionaires.

Another idea came to mind based on my experience during my training at RAAF Base Pearce in Bullsbrook, WA.

The Taiwanese Airforce had many airstrips all over the island, and it would be ideal to use one of those as our training base. We needed the authority to fly from the military administration, and a plan was hatched.

It took a while to get the proper introductions. Still finally, I had an interview, more like an audience, with the top military brass in charge of Taiwan Air Defence. He was a pleasant, elderly gentleman who patiently listened to what I proposed without interruption. I tried to sell the point that our gliding club could be an excellent opportunity to train future air cadets for the air force with no cost involved on their part. All we would need was to share the use of an airstrip, preferably close to Taipei, for easier access for would-be members working in that city.

My pride in being able to come up with such a brilliant plot was pricked quickly. There was no discussion about any details; I was kindly invited to step a little closer to look at a large wall map. Here the mighty size of mainland China was clearly shown next to the tiny island of Taiwan. Air Defence was anxious about a possible invasion by China and had to be ready at all times to launch fighter planes into the air if required. Any other operation on their airfield could disrupt their fighting readiness. There was no way we could get permission to run a gliding club even with the best intention to train local air cadets.

Once again, one of my dreams got busted.

Only a few years later, I visited Taiwan again, and a friend invited me for a flight in an ultra-light aircraft he owned. It seemed there had been a drastic change to government policies since my departure. The locals had taken advantage of that with gusto.

Sure enough, we had to take off from a dry rice paddy, but the initial bumpy run quickly became airborne. It was a bizarre situation sitting in such a contraption flying a few hundred feet about the ground. The ultra-light comprised a simple metal frame with canvass wings attached. The open seating was comparable to a couple of garden chairs, with a control stick and two rudder paddles to operate. One lever controlled the engine, which was mounted on the back of the frame, turning a small propeller to push us forward. That way, we could gain speed to get into the air and stay there.

The scenic flight was amazing. Plenty of rice paddies below and a few tiny houses in the middle of the fields. We found a strange construction past a little mountain that almost looked like the top of an aircraft carrier. I was told some local enthusiasts built this concrete deck along the hill to have a base for their flying operation. It turned out to be the wrong decision, which soon became apparent.

The whole new flying circus was not regulated. Any keen person with some money could get himself into one of those machines and learn some basics from another madman, and off they went to show their skills. Unfortunately for them, the concrete platform proved deadly for several of them.

The hill created a lot of wind turbulence. Coming in to land on the top was the aim, but a few inexperienced adventurers did not allow for constantly changing conditions.

They were coming to the landing strip with insufficient height and got pushed down and hit the side of the thick concrete construction. It did not take long before the local folklore blamed the site of the landing strip for all the mishaps.

As usual, cemeteries usually are on hills for various reasons. The additional bonus in Taiwan was that no rice paddy was used up for this purpose. This monstrous concrete landing strip was constructed for the same reason next to a cemetery to save land, but the cultural or spiritual aspect was totally ignored.

Shortly after these incidents, the government changed their open policy to introduce strict rules again, and this Wild West style flying stopped. The concrete monster on the hillside was converted into a go-cart racing track with no further incidents recorded.

In 1980, when I left Taiwan for Singapore, I faced another period of adjustment and hard work to get the local company into shape. My only flying was done as a passenger in large commercial aircraft to many destinations in Asia. It was all exciting, but it was not quite the same as being in command of a small plane.

Finally, I learned about the local flying club operating out of Seletar Airport, next to the stretch of water dividing Singapore from Malaysia. Training began again in a Cessna 150 and involved many take-offs and landings on this airfield, used for smaller planes operated by charter companies. Every time we came into land, I had a feeling of *déjà vu*. The landing strip was slightly uphill, and to land there, one had to come in over the sea, aim for the landing spot and roll up the hill for a stop. Every time I aimed at the landing point, I saw this grey seawall looming at me, which had to be cleared first before landing. This wall reminded me very much of the big concrete construction in Taiwan, and I made very sure to have sufficient height over that point before touching down.

Flying was not that difficult for me, but the radio traffic associated with flying in Singapore differed from Australia.

Singapore had five airports crammed onto this tiny island. Changi Airport had just been upgraded to become an international airport, and Paya Lebar became the Air Force base again. Then there were two airfields on the western side of Singapore used by fighter planes or helicopters. All these activities had to be monitored on the radio, restricted fly zones to be observed; there was a lot to do in the small cockpit, and the joy of flying was slightly reduced. To make it even more interesting, flying north would get you into Malaysian air space, which was only allowed if you landed there to go through strict immigration procedures. I really missed our more relaxed gliding activities in Australia.

Pressure built up for me again. During too many business trips around Asia, I felt pushed to get flying lessons on the few weekends I was at home with no other commitments. The final decision to stop training in Singapore came after another solo training flight out of Seletar.

After take-off, I had to switch the radio frequency to the traffic control frequency monitoring the whole traffic over the island. I could not go very far as the airspace designated for training was only three miles from the Airfield. I had a pleasant flight, went through the routine manoeuvres and felt reasonably competent in what I was doing. When the allocated hour was over, I turned back to the airfield and switched to the local radio frequency of Seletar tower. My call to advise of my intention to join the circuit was not answered. I tried again, with the same result. A slight panic ensued; it is not good to hang around the sky with so much air traffic in all directions and not have the assurance of traffic control to safely guide you back to earth. I switched back to the island frequency, and all was in order. Going back to the local tower frequency, I experienced the same problem, no communication. What on earth was the problem? Maybe the air traffic controller quit his job, went to the toilet or had a cup of tea? I made one more call and joined the circuit but kept a sharp lookout in all directions to make sure that I was not on a collision course with another aircraft.

On landing, I cleared the seawall with ample safety height and rolled to the flying club hangar with a thin film of sweat over my eyebrows. I really did not need that kind of excitement on the weekend. My daily activity running the company provided me with plenty of opportunities to prove my abilities.

When I told them my story, the flying club inspected the aircraft and found that the operating switch on the radio had some problems; the local tower frequency could not be connected. Well, I was relieved somehow; at least the total failure to communicate correctly was not my fault. The fact remained that I put too much pressure on myself. My family and the job had to come first, so I decided to end my flying training in Singapore.

The family returned to Perth to settle down in 1984. For me, that meant I had a chance to get back into gliding with the Narrogin Gliding Club, which kept me sane on weekends after turbulent days every week trying to build up my own little enterprise.

The required check flight to get my legal status to fly solo did not pose any problem, and I was back in the air. Although my Assistant Instructor Licence was not up to date, I still had my endorsement to fly with passengers, which I did as often as possible. Many friends and visiting family trusted me to take them on a joy ride in one of the twin-seater planes. It seemed everybody enjoyed the flights. For me, the most gratifying result was that none of my passengers got sick in flight as I tried to adjust my flying habits to suit the mentality of the person with me. Yes, the mentality is correct, as any fear of flying is mainly in the head and has nothing to do with a physical affliction (that would only result from mental pressure or anxiety).

The club had increased their fleet during the past years, and it was a pleasure to take flights in different single-seater gliders and experience extended flights in a more advanced type of plane. The highlight of the year was

Pre-take-off checks

Landing after a cross-country flight

A very happy pilot

always our expedition to the Stirling Ranges. Equipment, fuel drums for the tow plane and gliders had to be ferried to the simple airstrip we had carved out of a paddock years ago. Accommodation had significantly improved as the farmer's family, who owned the land, had developed a modern caravan park with onsite vans, little A-shaped cottages and a more extensive building housing showers, toilets and a covered outdoor space which served as a common kitchen and dining area.

These conveniences helped greatly to give us more time to fly and make the best use of the time we spent down there during the school holidays. A few members brought their children along, and off-days were used to go for hikes up to Bluff Knoll or climb another peak in the area. It was not uncommon to see a group of people on top of the cliffs getting excited when a couple of gliders swooped over their heads, having a good look at them.

Unfortunately, the flying fun did not last very long. After only two years, I had to move again but enjoyed around 100 flights and over 60 hours of flying. Enough to be current and have an incentive to continue to be an absent member of the gliding club for the next 18 years. Brief holidays in WA enabled me to have a few flights every year, but they were mainly refresher flights and taking passengers for a brief ride. It kept me interested, but it was not really advancing my skills.

My time in Hong Kong and Indonesia ended as we had plans to retire eventually in Perth. The timing was almost perfect; I still could work for the company for another four years in Perth with regional responsibilities in Asia, which required me to visit a lot of places every year. But it also gave me plenty of time to get back into flying in Narrogin, this time with the knowledge I would not have to leave again.

I realised I was a bit rusty and decided to join the training programme again to make sure I was up to date on new rules and regulations in aviation. The actual flying was OK, it is like hopping back on a bicycle after many years, and the ability to control the machine comes back quickly. I was checked and authorised for solo flights again after six weeks. The club acquired new gliders made of fibreglass, a far cry from what used to be the standard wood and canvas-covered plane. The old aluminium hull and wing of the Blanik were OK for training and fun flights, but the aircraft was getting the flight hours up and would be replaced soon.

Hilmer Geissler was an instructor with many hours of flying experience. He started his flying lessons years before in Germany, being a keen pilot when he came to Australia. We talked a lot about different planes and their capabilities and dreamed of owning one ourselves. We even looked at the latest models of electric motor gliders, which had impressive flying capabilities. The engine was only to be used for self-launching. Once the propeller was stowed away in flight, the plane was one of the most aerodynamic gliders available. It kept on being a dream; the investment was too great for us, as we did not particularly want to take out another mortgage on the house to come up with the finance.

One day Hilmer suggested following up on an advertisement he saw in a flying magazine. A pilot in NSW intended to sell his Nimbus 3 glider, which was designed and built in Germany. With attachment to the wings, they extended to 25 metres, which was considerably wider than the average gliders with 18 or 20 metres wingspan. The glide ratio was 58:1, which was at the top of the range. As a manufacturer, Schleicher had an excellent reputation for building amazing performance gliders, and we knew the Nimbus 2 as the previous model. The temptation was so great that we had to give it a go.

Hilmer, Rick and I formed a syndicate and decided to make an offer to the gentleman in Sydney. It was a fixed price; the offer was "as is where is", including a fully equipped trailer.

We had never seen the glider except in pictures, but research and talking to other members of the gliding fraternity convinced us that the glider was in good condition; it just needed an annual inspection and certification. So we confirmed we would buy it.

Now came the problem of how to get it back to WA. To move the trailer and glider on a truck or the railway would have been very expensive and needed a lot of coordination. A better solution was to go over there and tow the trailer back to Narrogin.

That posed another problem. Rick had his own business to run, and he could not get the time to travel to Sydney. Hilmer did not have a suitable vehicle to tow a glider all that distance, and he too had only a small time window to help. So it came down to me. I planned my trip to Sydney, packed plenty of water, nuts and fruit and started on the 4,000 km drive towards Sydney on my own. The decision to drive during daylight only was a safety measure. The Nullarbor is notorious for the number of accidents involving kangaroos.

That also meant I had to find accommodation within a reasonable day's drive to have a layover. The time became a little blur through driving ten to twelve hours every day, but I thought it might be good training for future long-distance flights in our glider.

I reached Sydney after 3½ days and bunked into a simple motel near the airport; I had to pick up Hilmer the following day when he would arrive by plane from Perth. He would share the driving on the way back, but first, we had to go to Campbelltown Airport, where the glider was situated, have a quick inspection, pay the owner and hook up the trailer to my Touareg to start the return journey.

A welcomed diversion to a little place near Orange gave us another short rest staying with Hilmer's sister. That also allowed us to check out the trailer and find that the wheel bearings were dry. The dirty job had to be done, take off the wheel, take out the ball bearings, clean them and squash enough grease into the cavities to keep an oxcart going for 100 years. I believed Hilmer that this had saved us from a very unpleasant accident on the way back; after all, the whole idea was to get our glider to Narrogin safe and sound.

Hilmer was eager to get back to assemble the glider as soon as possible. I insisted on sleeping at night, and the compromise was to get up early in the mornings. Just as well we did that. On packing up, I noticed I had a flat tyre. The damage in the tyre was visible, and I could use the special kit I had brought along to plug the hole. To pump up the tyre took a while because of its size and the small capacity of my on-board compressor. When we got going, all was OK. We looked forward to another day of driving. Thanks to a tyre pressure monitoring system, I realised the tyre lost quite a bit of air after travelling about 700 km. I pumped it up again to continue. When this became a frequent event, we needed to check what options we had. It was Friday afternoon, another 40 minutes to go to the next town of Southern Cross, which had a service station, but it was already 3 pm, and we were not sure when they would close. A slightly illegal speed got us into town by 3.30 pm to find the garage was just about to close for the weekend. Bless these country people; they are so accommodating and helpful. The tyre came off immediately; they pulled the rubber from the rim and found the original hole was still OK; my repairs had done the trick. But unknown to us, a new hole had been caused by a kangaroo bone, which had broken off and worked its way into the tyre from the inside, creating an even larger hole. The service people found a solution by inserting a large circular metal patch with a metal stem and closing the hole with additional sealant. What a great job by great people, and the final quote of only $30.00 for the job made our day.

Hilmer was a bit grumpy, and I decided to finish our journey as soon as possible. From Southern Cross, I drove straight to Narrogin late evening/night as I was sure that we would have no problems with kangaroos. All the roads crossing the country had fences to keep livestock in, which gave me the confidence to continue at night. It was close to midnight when we arrived in Narrogin and retreated in a hurry to our respective caravans to sleep a few hours.

My last thought before dropping off was the realisation that I had just finished a road trip of 8,000 km in 10 days. No wonder I was slightly elevated.

Hilmer did not waste any time the following day. I'd just got a cup of coffee when he pushed me to give him a hand to put the bits and pieces of the glider together.

What a beautiful sight when it was done. Sleek, long wings, the big tail elevator towering over the fuselage, and the cockpit looking inviting enough to hop in for a trial sitting. All moving parts seemed to follow the directions they were meant to, but we were required to pull everything apart again and check every pin and bearing to clean and grease. We had to inspect the fibreglass wings and attachments for any visible damage and polish the whole glider before issuing the yearly inspection certificate. Finally, we were ready to fly our Nimbus 3.

Narrogin became my favourite destination on my weekends. I finally had the time to have continuous practice in flying gliders. I could juggle work-related overseas trips to ensure I would not miss out on getting my fair share of flying times in our glider.

The gliding club had gained a new twin-seater plane, and all of us were trying hard to get some time in the air with that plane. It was of fibreglass

The Nimbus 3 at Narrogin

construction, comfortable to sit in the front or back, with an updated instrument panel catering for the more sophisticated pilots but easy to handle for the less experienced. However, once we all had our check flights, we got endorsed to fly the DG 505, and the struggle to have a flight in that glider became a challenge.

For me, it was of great importance that I could handle this modern flying machine; Hilmer insisted on giving me several introduction rides in the DG 505 before I was cleared by him to fly our syndicate-owned Nimbus 3. Maybe just as well.

What is the difference between one and the other plane, you may ask? Of course, they all have wings, a rudder and several control surfaces needed to control the flight. But, when it comes to the flying ability of each glider, there is a difference in the performance, and it is vital to become familiar with the specific peculiarities each aircraft displays in flight.

The DG 505 has a wingspan of 18 metres and a glide ratio of 40:1. That is considered an excellent performance for a twin-seater training aircraft. For me, it was almost a miracle compared to my first training aircraft, the Slingsby T31B, or what we called a flying brick with a glide ratio of 17:1.

Hilmer put me through my paces and ensured that every take-off and landing was perfect. I did not quite understand why he sought such perfection as I found the DG 505 very easy to fly. The wings were fairly high off the ground, the surface controls gave the pilot a firm control on the ground run, and in mid-air, and it was just simple fun.

After seven check rides, Hilmer finally nodded his reluctant approval for me to fly our Nimbus 3.

My preparation for my first solo flight in our glider took a bit of time. I needed to go through the checks several times to remember the sequence of events on take-off. Sitting in the comfortable cockpit, everything seemed much closer to the ground, including the wings sticking out on each side. The wings curve slightly towards the ground because the total wingspan was 25.5 metres. It soon became clear to me that total take-off concentration was needed to ensure a perfect ground run before we got enough speed for the actual take-off. It was imperative to keep the wings level as the wingtips moved only a few centimetres over the ground. If the wing dropped on the ground, it could result in a ground spin, causing damage to the glider if not picked up early. The first few metres were critical. A rapid increase in speed on launching was very important to get the air flowing over the wings, which created the up-lift and gave more substantial control to the pilot. The detailed and persistent instructions received from Hilmer became very useful.

Once in the air, I was still attached via the tow rope to the tow plane. We needed to climb to around 2,000 feet before I felt comfortable to release the tow rope and start flying the glider on my own. That meant I needed to find thermals to turn the glider within to gain altitude.

The enormous wingspan of the Nimbus 3 offered a new challenge to my ability to fly tight circles in a thermal. To initiate a turn, a combination of three actions is usually required. A combination of using the ailerons, rudder and correct speed is needed to get the glider to turn left or right. With the long wingspan of our Nimbus 3, it became quite a challenge to get into a turn before running out of the warm air bubble. A very sluggish turn was often the result, which meant I lost the bubble and had to look for a new thermal source. What I needed was more practice and more again.

I guess my first flight was not too bad. I clocked 32 minutes of air time, which was quite good considering the weather and my limited experience of throwing a 25.5 metre wingspan glider around the sky.

It was great to secure a seat in our own glider as only three pilots had to fight for it. I got plenty of air time to improve my performance and had many flights exceeding two and three hours. Whenever our glider was not available to me, I often secured the DG 505 for a solo or mutual flight, which included taking up many friends as passengers to introduce them to the great joys of flying. Some of them actually did like the flight.

Obviously, there is a big difference between a joy ride and more serious competition flights. The idea is to hone your skills by flying long hours and using the time to fly long distances in a respectable time, which translates into speed.

A task of 200 to 300 km was set for a day subject to the weather conditions. All the top guns went around those trips achieving speeds of 90 to 110 km per hour. But several times, they misjudged the change of weather and did not make it back to the airfield. They had plenty of choices to pick a paddock on a farm to land in, but that is where the problem lay. To decide to land in a field, you need to inspect the ground and make sure it is safe to land on. That usually should happen when are you around 2,000 feet with plenty of time to plan your landing circuit. Fences, power cables, livestock and piles of rocks can make landing a hazardous event. It is also recommended to check out the field's length to make sure the glider does not run short of a ground run before crashing into an obstruction. All that goes around in the head while calculating your height and converting it into the distance you can fly trying to find another thermal.

We all get trained for that, but I had a particular problem because of our Nimbus 3. The glider had a fantastic ability to stay in the air with a glide ratio of around 58:1, but it became a liability to land in a rough field if required. Long wingspan and low wings do not encourage a pilot to land in an unknown paddock. If the landing can be achieved with no damage, the immediate question turns to the retrieval from that paddock. If it is safe and long, it is possible to land a tow plane to pull the glider out. There is no ground crew to assist with holding the wing for take-off, and the wing of the glider has to be dragged on the ground until there is sufficient airflow to pick up the wing. Any minor obstacle can damage the glider as the force of impact multiplied by the leverage of the long wing could be dangerous.

The alternative was to bring in a ground crew and a trailer to dismantle the glider and move it back to the airfield for reassembly. Though the Nimbus 3 had great flying abilities, it had been built many years ago; it was an old-fashioned design and very cumbersome to pull apart and put together again. Heavy wing pieces had to be handled, and the fuselage needed at least three people to push into the trailer, followed by six pieces of the dissembled wings. To put it all together was a nightmare, exacerbated by the cumbersome need to secure any internal control connection with safety pins in dark, small areas where no light could shine on the delicate operation. It was literally touch and feel to confirm that everything was correctly in place.

Now you know why I was hesitant to follow other brave pilots who took quite a few risks trying to compete in the competitions, many of them out landing. That was not for me. Having said so, I took to cross-country flights on my own without the pressure of the competitors, which meant I could control my action without feeling I was a failure.

One particular flight comes to mind. On a day in January 2010, the weather forecast showed all the signs of a boomer day for flying. A cool night with scorching conditions during the day promised intense thermal activities, which got everybody excited and planning for long flights begun. What they did not mention particularly was that this type of weather is associated with quite violent disturbances in the air, which could be very discouraging closer to the ground. The top pilots donned their oxygen masks and plenty of sun cream and took off as soon as they thought the time was right. A couple of them did not make it on the first attempt to go on the task; the rough thermal activities near the ground did not go high enough to sustain a reasonable height to fly off on the task.

Once the hectic activities died down a bit on the launch pad, I got our Nimbus 3 ready. The launch was one of the roughest rides I ever had in a glider. Once off the ground, it seemed that the wind tried to turn me upside down and, with the slow reaction of the control panels, it became a matter of anticipating the next bumper and reacting before it actually happened. The tow plane before me tended to suddenly jump into the air, dragging me on the tow rope behind him. By the time I was back into the station just below his tail, a sudden downdraught would pull the tow plane down, leaving me hanging onto the tow rope, being well above his tail. Determined as I was, I did not let go until I was up at 2,000 feet.

There was no way I would have a second attempt to launch under those conditions; it was not pleasant at all.

The rest of the flight made history for me. Once up above 5,000 feet, the air became a little more stable, and from there on, it was just like a ride in an elevator. We climbed almost consistently at three to six knots per minute, and soon, I was up at 8,000 feet. At that height, I could fly a long distance with the excellent glide ratio our Nimbus 3 had. I took off to complete at least part of the task, losing height on the straight flights but picking up another thermal whenever I thought it was time to gain more height. The trees and maybe the occasional farmhouse became tiny below, and I realised I had climbed to 11,400 feet. It is not a good idea to hang around at that height without an oxygen supply. The brain starts to go a bit funny after being starved of sufficient oxygen, and it becomes more evident with greater heights. That is why aviation rules require oxygen systems in aircraft flying above 10,000 feet I had no oxygen rigged in our glider. I made sure not to get into trouble by pulling the plug and using the air brakes in the wing to reduce my height quickly. As far as I remember, I had no side effects other than those I already had before I took up gliding.

That day I spent over three hours in the air and flew only 270 km, but came down as a happy chap ready for a rewarding beer.

The dream of glider pilots is to achieve a long distances flight of 1,000 km or more. The best weather conditions for such an undertaking exist in Namibia, Africa.

Every year, a small group of international glider pilots arrive in Namibia to attempt the perfect flight. Specialist logistic companies provide the transport of gliders in containers to the established clubs in Africa. The owners can prepare and train to understand the weather pattern and the terrain and plan their flight, including elaborate safety measures. The flight routes are planned over vast areas of dry bushland where there is little hope of getting quick help in case of an unscheduled out-landing in the middle of nowhere.

Hilmer and I started planning a trip to Namibia to join the merry band of pilots in an attempt to obtain our 1,000 km distance goal. Many details had to be checked out, licences and insurance problems to be looked at.

Well, we had to drop our grand plans. Hilmer didn't seem keen anymore, and it was only a few months later that we found out the reason. Health was never an issue for Hilmer, but his life was turned upside-down when he was diagnosed with a tumour which could not be operated on. He had been given a few months, maximum of one year, before the inevitable end was predicted.

He put his affairs in order. After selling his light aircraft, he had to find a suitable buyer for his share in our glider. Another member of NGC was very interested, and ownership changed to Brian, a very experienced instructor and tow pilot.

We celebrated Hilmar's 70th birthday in Kings Park with family and friends to say farewell to a great guy.

Hilmer (left) and David (right) have been the most influential persons in my gliding experience

David, a Master Mariner, introduced me to gliding when he suggested joining the RAAF Base Pearce gliding club back in 1971. We spent many hours, even days together, operating the winch for launching at Pearce, pushing gliders into position, having our training together in both clubs, and flying together on many occasions in the years to come.

My experience with Hilmer came a few years later when I returned from overseas. He was an exceptional pilot with over 50 years of flying experience to pass on to willing students. He was short on tolerance when he encountered people who were a bit slow on the uptake, but otherwise one of the most knowledgeable gliding instructors I have experienced.

It was not too long afterwards when Hilmer passed away; his ashes were taken to the Narrogin Gliding Club. His last wish was to have his ashes scattered over the Narrogin Airfield from the beloved Nimbus 3. Our third partner in the syndicate, Rick, did the honour fly-past in our glider and got the contents of the urn out of the small window into the air above the crowd attending the memorial.

Brian was a very valuable new member of our syndicate. I had minimal experience in the maintenance of gliders; I just knew how to fly them.

The Nimbus 3 in flight

Rick was very knowledgeable, but his work commitment made it difficult for him to spend much time at the club.

Every year the glider had to be pulled apart, cleaned, oiled or greased. Every part had to be inspected in case of any faults in the wings, fuselage or the control mechanism. We picked the winter months to do this work as there was not much flying because of adverse weather.

The yearly expedition to the Stirling Ranges continued with part of the club's fleet ferried across to the paddock next to the now flourishing caravan park near the entry to Bluff Knoll Drive.

The experience of flying close to or above the Stirlings is hard to describe. Exhilaration and joy, but with high concentration to make every flight a safe experience in the different surroundings of the mountain area.

The launch behind the tow plane could take up to 10 minutes before reaching the top of Bluff Knoll. Once released, we needed to find out the local sources of thermal activities, which could be larger rocks being warmed up by the sun or just using the updraught created by the wind when hitting the bottom of the rocky slopes. In good conditions, we had

Tow plane coming back from Bluff Knoll

Glider coming in to land from Bluff Knoll

no problem staying up for a long time, just flying back and forth in front of the Bluff.

In strong conditions, we would fly over the plateau to explore the other side of the rocks but had to be wary of downdraughts which could prevent us from getting back over the top. If that happened, the only way to find a paddock for safe landing would be about 50 km further south, towards Albany.

I was never keen to get into such a situation; why spoil a perfectly good day by taking unnecessary risks?

Towing towards Bluff Knoll

Bluff Knoll in sight

Level with Bluff Knoll

Approaching the landing strip

Happy pilots after an exciting day

My daughter, Melissa, was keen to become a commercial pilot. To test her ability, I suggested joining NGC and learning what it was all about.

She took to flying like a duck to water and became a solo pilot on her 15th birthday, which was before she could get a driver's licence.

She was keen to start her commercial pilot's licence training as soon as possible. In principle, I was happy to sponsor her. But I had learned from past contacts with airline pilots that their profession is fickle, relying heavenly on their mental and bodily fitness. A slight ailment impairing their ability to fly could jeopardise their career, and they would have to start again in another profession.

Plenty of arguments later, Melissa agreed to finish her university studies first, to have a base if flying did not work out for her. Three years later, with a BSc to her credit, I sponsored her expensive training to become a commercial pilot. She advanced rapidly and became an instructor with the Royal Aero Club in Jandakot, with an excellent chance to be scouted by an international airline and trained further to fly jet aircraft.

For various reasons that never happened. Melissa took up more studies and ended up with another degree as an Engineering Graduate and left the aviation industry altogether.

It seems I had prophesied my dilemma years before.

A cataract operation on both eyes improved my vision back to 20/20. Unfortunately, a side effect of getting a dry eye resulted in tears which slightly blurred my vision on my right side. Legally it was no problem; I could fly as long as I had a driver's licence. It just did not feel right to me; I did not want to jeopardise anybody flying near me in case I could not spot them clearly and cause them to worry about space separation.

My flying ambitions were put to rest. However, I insisted on completing my annual check ride with a qualified instructor, which I passed without a hitch on 12th July 2014.

That was my last flight as a pilot, and I always resisted the offer of my friends in NGC to join them for a joyride; I just did not want to feel the yearning to start flying again; any such attempt would have to be short-lived.

Great memories of flying and great friends to remember; I am really grateful for my experiences over many years.

Now I am making paper planes to test my skills and feel envious of the pilots at RAAF Base Pearce doing their training flights over my head at The Vines golf course.

Once upon a time, in a country far across the seas, old and young men, dressed in leather pants, gathered to observe an age-old German tradition.

Fairy Tale

It was late morning when they sat down, discussed the weather and commenced the celebration of *Brotzeit*. Copious measures of beer made from wheat were consumed, and a simple mix of sausage meat mixed with onions, vinegar and cheese was served with freshly baked bread. All this centred on the masterpiece; a white vegetable commonly known as radish was expertly cut into never-ending thinly sliced spirals and presented on a stick to hold it all in place. Delicious salt had to be applied to make it even tastier. With the growing thirst, the flow of beer increased, to the great satisfaction of the innkeeper.

Some of these men had braved the seas to visit strange countries and fell in love with their new surroundings. Until they felt they were missing something. So one day, one of them invited a neighbour to celebrate with him, which appeared to be a great way of becoming friends. So the neighbour decided other friends should be educated in the ways of the odd men dressed in leather pants. The next time the celebration took place, there was a strange assembly of persons around the table: the original leather pants man came from a faraway place called Bavaria, the neighbour hailed from further north, a place known as Prussia. The newcomers represented a wide range of cultures and languages. A strong man born and bred in Uganda and educated in Great Britain, a grey-haired old gentleman from Wales who travelled the world in his little Austin 7 for many years, and there was an Italian, born in Australia, married to a Swiss, who had sworn not to miss out on any good celebration which ended by smoking a good Cuban cigar.

The powers of *Brotzeit* did the rest; a new group of believers in ancient traditions was created, to the benefit of humankind. The word has been spread, and there are signs that many outsiders are to be introduced to this noble tradition, even if they do not wear leather pants anymore.

A small item that jogs a memory of a great friend and my very brief attempt to read Latin.

A Little Thing with a Big Impact

I knew the gentleman for several years before he became my boss in a large, international organisation. Dr Hans Ebert was a member of the Board of Directors in the Head Office in Germany; I was based in Hong Kong, looking after the Asian Region.

I need to explain a bit about the culture in Germany. Academics are very much revered, to such an extent that it is almost a requirement to have a PhD to join any Board of Directors. Either that, or a healthy measure of Vitamin C, where the C stands for connections. Once the PhD is added to the list of qualifications, the honouree title of Doctor is given to the person regardless of the dissertation's subject. Convention would demand that this Doctor's wife would be addressed as Mrs Doctor So-and-so, even though she may never have seen a university from the inside.

Dr Ebert and I had many meetings; we travelled together all over Asia and became quite friendly. But as he was my boss and had a PhD, I had to follow the laws of courtesy and always address him as Dr Ebert, even if we were hanging around half-drunk in a bar in Korea or some other place during our travels. He never addressed me by my first name. However, he would introduce me as Folker whenever we met the local business people.

During one of our more private discussions, Dr Ebert mentioned he had problems with his hairstyling. I had to laugh; what hairstyling was he referring to? As long as I had known him, he always had a crew cut, pristine and neat. I suggested following my example and using a dog grooming brush in the future. He took that advice but could not find such a brush anywhere in Germany. Therefore, I was required to bring one of those items to my next meeting with Dr Ebert.

Years later, Dr Ebert retired, but we kept in touch, communicating via emails and telephone. On one of his birthdays, I realised Dr Ebert was six months younger than me. Well, that gave me an opportunity to play a trump card. I did not have to follow convention, since he was not my boss anymore. My card was that I simply claimed the right, as an older person, to invite him to drop the formalities and call each other by our first names.

Dr Ebert became Hans by writing to me he would respect an elder's right and granted me my wish. He finished by quoting a Latin phrase which I presumed meant the same.

That is when I became a short-term scholar of Latin. I needed to find out what this bit of Latin meant. Here is a brief note of what the translation meant and where it came from.

"The idea of a king or other nobleman having the right to sexually entertain a woman on her wedding night is known as **jus primae noctis**, a Latin phrase translating to 'right of the first night'. The concept was often extended to allow noblemen to take the virginity of any lower-class woman in their territory."

Initially, Hans was a little embarrassed but he conceded that he had lost a lot of his Latin and apologised for the implied meaning. We laughed at that for many years until Hans had to leave this earth, far too early.

Every time I use this little hairbrush, I remember Hans and the good years working together.

It was a beautiful, sunny but crisp day. Tee-off on hole 10; the three golfers drove their balls forward on the long fairway and walked towards their location.

A Golfing Story

Two balls had landed close to each other on the side of the fairway, shining very white in the bright sun. Two crows landed close by and hopped close to the ball in front to have a good look at it.

Golfer Fred jokingly said to his mate John, "Look! The crows are going to steal your ball!"

As if on command, a third crow arrived and positioned itself close to crow number two. Then crow number three lifted its left leg and pushed crow number two slightly sideways so it could get closer to the ball. Yes, it used its left leg to push its accomplice out of the way, not its wing.

A short reconnaissance and crow number three picked up the ball in his beak. Then he took off heavily on a short, low flight towards a scrubby area 50 metres away, with crows number one and two in hot pursuit. The ball was dropped, and the group had another inspection of what they most likely thought of as a tasty egg for their consumption.

By that time, Fred realised it was actually his ball which had been nicked, and not wanting to end this hole as a loser, he ran towards the crows to recover the ball. Crow number three picked up the ball again, but at this stage it must have been under stress at being chased by a big, burly man and decided for a quick get-away rather than a heavy take off. The ball was left behind, and Fred duly placed it back on the fairway. The game continued.

The look and taste of green olives bring up powerful memories.

Something Small

First, a great pain in the neck. Taking a long trip with my friend Alan, we camped in an olive grove in what was then Yugoslavia. It looked inviting, sunset shaded by the prolific trees, our tent set upright in the middle of a little forest of olive trees.

The idyllic situation became unbearable at night. Sleeping on the ground with only a thin floor covering between us and the olives which had fallen off the trees turned out to be torture without relief. These olives tended to be very hard, big and pressed into the back whichever way one turned. A night hard to forget.

Second, early mornings on the southern coast of Greece are not always welcome. For lack of camping grounds, we were invited to put up our tent right in front of a house alongside the waterfront. A friendly family with many children lived in the place, as we found out too early the next morning. We were woken up by lots of giggling and shuffling and dogs barking. The hospitable family wanted to welcome us with their traditional morning snack of green olives. I had never tasted olives before in my life, and here I forced myself to appear to be thankful for the gift by eating copious quantities of that green fruit in front of the bunch of children. The strange taste, slightly oily, was something I could never get rid of. This happened again on the second morning, and I decided I would never, ever touch this poison again.

LAST WORDS

A recent meeting of the 'Past Tense' group was enriched by the insight of the WIR (Writer in Residence), Rashida Murphy.

Ego Trip

Rashida posed a question to all aspiring writers: "why you want to write a book?" My answer, in two words, was, "Ego-trip", which earned me the accolade of being one of the few people who are honest about it.

Well, I thought about it a bit more and saw that the connotation of this was that I wanted to blow my own trumpet. How could anybody write their own memoirs without mentioning him or herself on at least a few pages? After all, the word 'ego' (Latin) means 'I' in English and 'Ich' in German. So the logical conclusion is that you write about yourself, trying to introduce your life to a specific or a wider audience as it may be.

Rashida introduced the idea that she has to be depressed to get the motivation to write. That does not sit with me; I need to be in good spirits to get my brain to develop ideas and put something on paper. Doing so introduces a little of my weird sense of humour into whatever situation is appropriate.

Growing up in a time that presented many challenges and, to a degree, hardships, we had to make the best of things. It helps to be young and ignorant, and as kids we mostly had a good time. It later emerged that we were not privileged and had to work harder to become successful in life. Education was limited to High School for various reasons. Therefore, no PhD or other fancy letters behind my name to show for it. Life takes over, and there is little time to reflect on all that until retirement. You look back and see that there are many stories worth exploring further, which automatically leads to other meanings of ego. Self-esteem, self-respect, self-confidence and yes, self-conceit to a degree.

No one is perfect, but I don't think there is any harm in feeling good about what one has done in life, such as family, work achievements, and even ticking off items on the bucket list. But, of course, that must automatically introduce ego again. Still, in my mind, it does not have any effects which could be obnoxious to a third party. If a reader does not like what and how I write, that is his privilege. In my opinion, he would miss out on a novel experience, and it is his loss (I say this with my tongue firmly in cheek).

Bottom line: I do not see that one can distance oneself from the ego when writing a memoir. It is part of the process, and why would anybody write about himself if he does not feel good about it?

So memoirs are all about ego, and it works for me.

www.ingramcontent.com/pod-product-compliance
Lightning Source LLC
Chambersburg PA
CBHW061139010526
44107CB00069B/2990